New Business Models for the Knowledge Economy

New Business Models for the Knowledge Economy

WENDY JANSEN, WILCHARD STEENBAKKERS
and HANS JÄGERS

Routledge
Taylor & Francis Group

LONDON AND NEW YORK

First published 2007 by Gower Publishing

Reissued 2018 by Routledge
2 Park Square, Milton Park, Abingdon, Oxon OX14 4RN
711 Third Avenue, New York, NY 10017, USA

Routledge is an imprint of the Taylor & Francis Group, an informa business

First issued in paperback 2018

A Library of Congress record exists under LC control number: 2006103149

Notice:
Product or corporate names may be trademarks or registered trademarks, and are used only for identification and explanation without intent to infringe.

Publisher's Note
The publisher has gone to great lengths to ensure the quality of this reprint but points out that some imperfections in the original copies may be apparent.

Disclaimer
The publisher has made every effort to trace copyright holders and welcomes correspondence from those they have been unable to contact.

ISBN 13: 978-0-815-39063-3 (hbk)
ISBN 13: 978-1-138-61994-4 (pbk)
ISBN 13: 978-1-351-15272-3 (ebk)

Contents

List of Figures

List of Tables

Preface

Business models are widely discussed. We encounter the concept everywhere, in academic literature, in the press, in board rooms and throughout organisations. After the first shake-out of the dot-coms, people began to ask themselves what caused such a large number of business failures. It was not just the reversing economy. The reason why many organisations failed is that they had no clear idea of what they wanted to accomplish. And an adequate fine-tuning between adopted strategy, management, business processes and information technology was frequently lacking. This brought the concept of the business model to the centre of attention, and research into the subject has become topical and relevant. The current revival of the economy and the fact that not only have many 'traditional' organisations set foot on the electronic highway, but also dot-com enterprises are showing healthy profits, has not diminished the interest in business models, but in fact has intensified it. So, what business models are effective in the network economy? What are the components of an effective business model? How can organisations determine if they have chosen an effective business model and (if not) how can they migrate to a new one? From what perspectives can, or should you consider the concept of business models?

These questions have been the subject of study of a research group of PrimaVera. PrimaVera is a forum of the University of Amsterdam, where academic researchers, students and business people meet. The objective of PrimaVera is to promote dialogue between these groups, to search for knowledge and to identify innovative and breakthrough ideas. The ideas around business models in this book are derived from and based on many inspiring and challenging discussions held in this research group. We thank the participants for their very valuable contributions. These ideas have been elaborated in a smaller group, consisting of Henri Melger, Jos Maassen, Henk van der Hooven and Vincent Jentjens. This group has had a major impact on the development of the typology and has created an inspiring and 'fun' learning environment for us, for which we are very grateful. Henri, especially, has our gratitude because not only has he given shape to an important type of business model, the Foyer, but he has also provided us with insightful feedback on the overall text of the book. And last but not least, our special thanks to our 'translator' Tom de Graaf. He not only translated this book, but scrutinised the content of the chapters. Through his critical and analytical comments, he helped us to rethink and rewrite a great number of our assumptions and suggestions. His contribution has led to major improvement of our typology.

In this book we do not offer any simple 'plug and play' solutions or a practical guide for the implementation of a certain business model. Our objective has been to develop a model that helps managers, consultants and employees of an organisation to position their organisation and to consider the need for a transformation towards a new business model. We believe the real challenge for organisations is to determine the situation in which it finds itself, to analyse and describe the opportunities it presents and to develop possible business models to fully exploit these opportunities. The purpose of the typology is to encourage reflection about the future and about the consequences of the choice of a certain business model. The value of the typology lies in the way in which organisations can find clues for changes in their desired direction.

We realise that a lot of aspects of business models are not new. In the theories of Adam Smith, Frederick Taylor and their many successors, we find elements of what we now call business models. But that does not mean that there is nothing new under the sun. The enormous opportunities of our network age lead to new intelligent combinations with existing business concepts. We are convinced that the typology described in this book will add a new dimension to the discussion about business models.

CHAPTER 1

Introduction

In recent years there has been frequent mention of the term 'business model'. Unexpected developments in organisations working in the network economy have led to curiosity about their business models. Managers and academics have speculated about which business models have led to spectacular successes and which have been used by organisations that have withered and died. The question of which business models are effective in this age of fast and dramatic change clearly occupies the minds of many. The objective of this book is to propose a framework for business models. Three new types of business models are presented based around the concepts of 'customisation', 'innovation' and 'authenticity'. Understanding and designing new business models are important parts of the role of modern managers and consultants.

A Golden Age?

Schumpeter, the Austrian economist, found that technological revolutions begin in clusters. These clusters ultimately change not only the way people do business, but the very dynamics of society. A technological revolution begins with one or more technologies that enable the existence of the new cluster. When the first successes are made public, technical people will start up small business, based on the new ideas. A fierce competition develops in this early and turbulent phase. Government regulation is largely absent, and as successes mount in a technical free-for-all, the promise of extraordinary profit looms. That is the moment the general population begins to speculate. The middle phase of a technological revolution sees a sustained buildout or golden age of the technology, during which it becomes the engine of growth for the economy. Large organisations reign, and the period is one of confidence and prosperity. In the last phase, the technology is mature. It has saturated its possibilities, production moves to places on the periphery, and complacency sets in. Entrepreneurs are starting to browse the market, looking for new possibilities. The time is ripe for a new revolution. Naturally, the exact phases and what happens in them are debatable. But what interests me is the pattern of speculative exuberance, followed by a crash and then a strong buildout period. If this pattern applies to the information era, then we are not observing the end of the information revolution. On the contrary, we have only gone a short way, and the Golden Age has yet to arrive.

(Arthur 2002).

SEARCHING FOR A NEW BUSINESS MODEL

When Chesbrough and Rosenbloom (2002) were searching the web in May 2000, they found 107,000 references to the term 'business model'. In June 2004 they found 2,130,000 mentions on Google, while in July 2006 the number of references had increased to 602,000,000. The popularity of the concept of business model has grown at a steady pace with the opportunities for businesses to profit from the changing environment, developments in information technology (IT) and the Internet. Few concepts in business today are as widely discussed and as seldom systematically researched as the concept of business models (Weill et al. 2005).

Business opportunities are there to be exploited if organisations opt for an effective business model. But managers, consultants and academic researchers remain unsure of what type of business model to adopt, and in which situations it will be effective. It is important to realise that there is not just one effective business model for the Internet era. Specific contexts, such as different organisational environments and strategies for added value may lead to different forms of effective business models.

TRENDS

The development of Western society has been characterised by increasing individualisation. This means that customers no longer wish for standard products or services, but increasingly demand customised service. As a consequence of the growing individualisation, an increasing need for personal involvement is acknowledged. This involvement should be based on authenticity, which implies that not just a mere illusion of a shared identity is offered, simply for the purposes of marketing, but that there is a real sense of community. Never before have individuals been united in so many (virtual) communities, working together at a global level.

The combination of an explosive growth and cheap transfer of knowledge, especially via the Internet, has created fertile ground for virtually unlimited innovation. This innovation is the response to the public's growing demand for products and services that are new and advanced.

These trends force many organisations to deliberately incorporate concepts like authenticity, involvement and innovation into their strategy. The business model approach we propose in this book should help you to focus the strategy of your organisation and to structure its processes and IT in a way that they become more efficient, more flexible and more responsive to customer demand. Such an approach is designed to make forecasting of future scenarios possible and leads to competitive advantage in this complex world.

TO WHOM IS THIS BOOK ADDRESSED?

> *During a conference in fall 1998, a consultant employed in a large consulting firm presented his audience with the following anecdote. Two students approached a venture capitalist with a concept for a dot-com business. Intrigued by what he heard in the first few minutes of the students' presentation, this man asked them whether they have a business plan. Oh, did they ever! The students emphatically retrieved a business plan from their pockets – all three hand-written pages – and the deal was done. A handshake later, cash was promised. Soon the money was delivered and a dot-com was born. This was a deal typical of that period.*

This book is not about dot-com organisations that were founded to function only in the digital world of the Internet. A much broader perspective is adopted, which makes the principles applicable to any organisation. Some examples from the dot-com industry will be presented however, since inconsistencies between the strategy of the organisation and design of the processes and IT application are often dramatically illustrated in this industry. The lack of effective business models has been a pervasive problem in starting Internet businesses.

OBSTACLES

The dot-coms were the pioneers that first tried to profit from the Internet through all sorts of new concepts. Since most dot-coms were founded for this purpose alone, they were not hindered by baggage from the past. After the first phase of the dot-com boom which included several amazing successes but many more spectacular failures, the 'second wave' followed with the advent of existing bricks and mortar organisations that decided to venture onto the Internet (Weill and Vitale 2001). During this second wave, increasing attention was given to the effectiveness of the existing business models and the choice of new business models. In this period, although a number of opportunities were certainly recognised, many organisations remained unenthusiastic about transforming their business models. The Internet was, and remains, in many cases, regarded as little more than an extra distribution channel.

Nowadays, doing business via the Internet, the vital role of IT in organisational processes and in customer relations, and the importance of network partners, are considered 'business as usual' for many organisations and individuals all over the world.

The question of choosing the most effective, flexible and inspiring business model, remains unexplored territory for many organisations. The reasons for this are complex. Organisations are often either organisationally or technologically oriented, but seldom both. Managers in these organisations have often gained their position because of successes with their own focused strategy. It is difficult to let go of these previous successes and to venture into new (unknown) territories (Dutta and Segev 1999).

A second obstacle is the fact that real innovation, such as the decision to apply a new business model, rarely produces short-term profits. The Return on Investment (ROI) is difficult to analyse. The IT infrastructure required for new business models often greatly exceeds the available IT budgets in many organisations. Many traditional organisations have not yet obtained the physical and IT infrastructures, the knowledge and skills, the culture and the leadership that are conditional to a successful transition to a new business model. Moreover, many organisations still have customers who prefer to do business the old-fashioned (familiar) way. Natural conservatism and an unwillingness to rock the boat keep the discussion about changing business models grounded; which often makes it difficult to develop a new business model within the organisation. For the same reason, some managers opt to found a new organisation that falls outside all structures of the existing one (Chesbrough and Rosenbloom 2002).

OBJECTIVE OF THIS BOOK

The concept of business models is relevant for all organisations. A business model tells a story of the business, focusing attention on how the pieces of the business fit together; with the strategic component of the model describing how the organisation differentiates itself in its approach to customers, partners and competition (Magretta 2002). Empirical research of the top 1000 firms in the USA shows that business models are a better predictor of financial performance than industry classifications and that some business models do, indeed, perform better than others (Weill et al. 2004). The concept of the business model fulfils an important function in current strategic thinking. There are only a few integrative strategy models that unite the finer aspects of strategy (resource bases, activities, structure, products and external factors). This makes the business model concept (which can be considered as such an integrative model) of great importance. Furthermore, the model is useful in explaining the relationship between IT and the strategy of the organisation. Therefore the business model concept is useful not just in the domain of (e-) business, but also to understand the impact of any IT application (Hedman and Kalling 2003). Finally, a business model can be seen and used as a means by which organisations can leverage technology to generate economic value (Chesbrough and Rosenbloom 2002). The failure of organisations to manage effectively in the face of technological change can be understood as the difficulty these organisations have in perceiving and then enacting new business models when technological change requires it.

The objective of this book is to provide managers with a foundation for further reflection on the choices for an effective new business model. The core of the book consists of a typology of business models that is introduced in Chapter 3 and developed in the following chapters. You may use our typology to understand the choices you need to make for your own business model.

PERSPECTIVES

The subject of business models can be viewed from multiple perspectives. Some of these will be discussed below. Out of these perspectives, the central one for this book is the design perspective.

TECHNOLOGICAL PERSPECTIVE

The technological perspective is often the dominant one because of the perception of the Internet as a technological application, one that has brought about irreversible changes in the world and in the way businesses function. We have found a consensus that a real breakthrough in technology creates the need for new organisational structures and processes and for new strategies to exploit the sources of competitive advantage. The strategies, structures and processes, that were appropriate for the previous technological regime, have become ineffective due to the technology breakthrough. Such changes pose different challenges for both start-up businesses and existing players. Where start-ups face the task of creating new organisations in order to exploit the new opportunities, existing businesses must change their present strategies, structures and processes and/or create new organisations to exploit these same opportunities. Technology alone will never lead to improvement of an organisation's performance. New, properly founded business models are necessary in order to employ a new technology effectively.

ECONOMICAL PERSPECTIVE

When people discuss changes associated with the technological revolution, the term 'network economy' frequently comes up. This refers to an economy in which individuals and organisations are part of a series of networks, in which information and communication technology increases productivity and changes the laws of supply and demand, scarcity and trade cycles. It differs from the traditional economy in that information can be reproduced indefinitely. Previously, overabundance meant devaluation of a product, nowadays, quite the opposite is true. The current abundance of information and ideas and the combination of this ubiquitous information can lead to new products and services, which can be widely distributed via multiple channels. The network economy uses 'soft' resources such as knowledge and the human tendency to solve problems, and turns them into smart products and processes that require less energy and resources. The essence of the network economy is 'connectivity'; everything is connected with everything and everyone; people, machines and networks. The combination of people, ideas and knowledge enables different configurations. Organisations need business models that are appropriate for the network economy. For instance, Internet users have drastically improved capabilities to organise themselves, which creates a whole new set of 'rules of engagement'. In the literature on business models, as well as in practice, this economical perspective is dominant, even more so than the technological perspective. The question 'how can money be made?' takes a central role (Rappa 2000, 2003; Timmers 1998). In Chapter 7, this perspective is explored in several interviews.

MARKETING PERSPECTIVE

Aside from developing new business models, many organisations require a change of culture in order to profit from the opportunities of the Internet. Thinking in terms of customers' needs instead of one's own takes a central role in this perspective. Marketing belongs to the economical perspective, but since many business models are described specifically from a marketing perspective, we have devoted a separate subsection to it.

The marketing perspective revolves around the customer. Customers no longer think in terms of products, but increasingly in terms of the activities they engage in to satisfy specific interests (Sawhney and Kaplan 1999). How should organisations deal with the customer if considered from the perspective of customer interests and experience? And how do organisations regard the customer when they use the Internet?

The Internet is a great influence on marketing thinking. Maintaining relations with individual customers has become much more of a possibility (Dutta and Segev 1999). Mass marketing and a distant contact with the customer are no longer appropriate in the light of current developments. In the old days, geographical diffusion, fragmentation of demand and transportation costs required intermediate levels of distribution, such as agents or retailers. Since the advent of the Internet, distance, space and location have become relative concepts. Thus, the search, evaluation, negotiation, payment and reception of products by customers can occur at various times and through various parties and channels. Instead of a single flow from organisation to agent to customer, there are now several flows, both informational and physical. While customers gain in diminished transportation costs (among other things), they may lose as a result of the increased costs and uncertainty of searching to find the right option amongst the hundreds available. In a number of new business models customers are presented with solutions to this problem. An example is Priceline, where 'you can set the price' you are willing to pay for a specific product or service (www.priceline.com).

SOCIOLOGICAL PERSPECTIVE

The sociological perspective considers general societal trends that lead or contribute to new business models. It suggests that social changes are at least as influential as technological or economical transformations. In a situation in which global monetary flows, power and images dominate, the search for identity becomes the main source of social sense-making for people. The desire for an authentic and meaningful existence has slowly become more pervasive (Taylor 1992). The modern preoccupation with identity and authenticity relates to the collapse of the classical social hierarchies. Originally, one's identity was mainly determined by one's social status. Acknowledgement and appreciation were dependent on position and role in society in the organisation within which you work, and the inherent social activities. With the decline of the paternalistic society, the rise of the middle classes and the changing labour- and ownership-relations, it has become unclear what defines your identity. These days identity is not determined by what you do, but by what you are, or believe yourself to be. Various foundations for the determination of your identity exist, following gender, ethnical or religious backgrounds (Castells 1 1998).

Another social transformation has taken place in the production factor of labour. Two fundamentally different kinds of labour can be distinguished. The first kind is labour for which no specific education and/or knowledge is required. This kind of labour has collective value, but individual people are replaceable by machines or other employees. The second kind is individual and indispensable labour, based on specific knowledge the working individual possesses. This second form is increasingly important (Castells III 1998).

These social transformations have caused a transition of power. The availability of education to a much larger proportion of the population than before has shifted the power from employers to employees. Employees are now to be treated as volunteers, who may (and will) get up and walk away at any time, taking with them all their human intellectual capital (Drucker 2001).

Analogous to this phenomenon, the power of organisations can be said to have shifted to customers. This is partly expressed in the economical perspective. The value of customers and employees, but the search for authenticity and identity as well, are of great significance in the formulation of business models.

DESIGN PERSPECTIVE

This book was not written from a single perspective, but considers business models from an integrated design approach. Naturally, aspects of the individual perspectives discussed above remain influential in the background of our chosen design approach. From a design perspective the focal point is structure; the way in which the activities in an organisation or network are organised into structures. These structures dictate the division of labour and regulate the governance of the organisation and/or network. The design approach considers the participants in these structures, such as the individuals in the organisation(s), but also the customers, suppliers and other stakeholders. This book addresses the design of an organisation from the perspective of business models. In a business model the choice of a strategy leads to a division of labour, but also to a specific arrangement for the structuring of activities and governance. The components of these business models are considered in mutual relation to each other and to the environment of the organisation or network. For this reason we have opted for the following definition of the concept business model for this book (Ethiraj et al. 2000).

> *A business model is a unique configuration of elements that consists of the strategy, technologies, and the coordination of the organisation. This configuration was formed to create value for the customers and thus to compete successfully in a certain market.*

A DEVELOPMENTAL VIEW

The configuration of elements in a business model results from specific perspectives on organisations and their goals. Over time, a clear trend can be discerned in the way organisations are regarded. The shifts in focus in design have been described by Handy (in Amidon 1997) in his so-called Sigmoid-curve (see Figure 1.1). The Sigmoid-curve is an S-shaped curve that illustrates the lifecycle of a product, an organisation or the progress of a civilisation. After a hesitant start-up of an organisation (product or civilisation), success arrives. But after another period of time the success decreases and the decline begins. Whether or not an organisation is capable of entering a new Sigmoid-curve before it reaches this point is an important aspect of the business model concept. Handy suggests that a critical turning point exists, when an organisation should try a new direction. The change of strategy and the accompanying drastic changes in the organisation should thus start, while the 'old' strategy still seems to be working properly. This change of direction demands competent leadership and a lot of courage. The problem is that it becomes increasingly difficult to begin a new curve when the effectiveness of the organisation is already displaying a downward trend. Figure 1.1 has been elaborated by Amidon (1997), who added two new levels: the value of giving attention to customers and the value of knowledge. In this book we added another level in this figure, namely the attention given to communities (Level VI). The subjects in Levels IV, V and VI are considered to be essential aspects of the network economy.

The first three levels of Figure 1.1 describe elements of the 'traditional' economy, resulting from the dominant ideology of economic rationalism. Bambury (2001) suggests that this ideology causes our lack of understanding of many developments in the Internet and e-commerce (electronic commerce). Economic rationalism ultimately reduces everything to economical value. But the Internet works differently from corporate business. In practice, developments are largely brought about by the users, many of whom are scientists, programmers, academics, librarians, intellectuals, political activists and artists. In most cases they are not representatives of businesses. They strive for different values than those which are purely economical. Sharing of information and knowledge is culturally appreciated, status is not determined by possessions and territory but by demonstrated expertise, reputation and the contribution made to the Internet or the Internet community. Bambury (2001) states that the interface between the economy of corporate business and the original Internet economy is essentially a clash of cultures.

Organisations that manage to incorporate elements of the 'softer' values such as sense of community, knowledge sharing and idealism into their business model, will perform better in the network economy than organisations with business models that are based solely on economic rationalism. In the

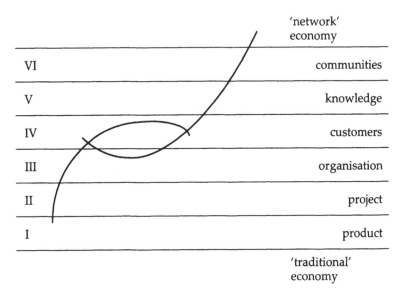

Figure 1.1   Sigmoid-curve

discussion of the three types of business models in this book we will return to these values for a thorough evaluation.

When you are reflecting on the point of the Sigmoid-curve at which you find your own organisation and whether your current business model is still adequate, you may find Figure 1.1 helpful. An important question is whether the organisation is still in the right 'business'. A business always concerns a border-crossing of activities, in which multiple actors, such as customers, suppliers and (network) partners, play important roles.

But who in the organisation finds the leadership and the courage to make a timely transition to the new curve? In the next section we suggest some questions which may help you to determine whether it is time to seriously consider a transition to a new curve.

A FEW QUESTIONS FOR MANAGERS

If you wish to generate a clear picture of the situation your organisation is in, and to assess the urgency of seriously considering a new business model, ask yourself the following questions:

- Why do existing customers choose my organisation instead of others? In other words, what added value (focus especially on the 'soft' values) does my organisation provide to customers?

- Do customers benefit from a developing interaction with each other and/or my organisation? Is the way in which they can use our product or service improved by what they learn from each other? What can the organisation learn from or through them?

- How does the customer's educational history influence their tendency to purchase this particular product or service? Does the organisation have information on this subject?

- What are the processes for which the customers need a solution? Can the organisation – possibly in co-operation with the customer or other organisations – provide additional alternative solutions?

- How is the product or service used? Has the company configured its expertise to the use, maintenance or phasing out of the product/ service in ways that might be of use to the customer?

- Who are the 'physical' and who are the online competitors? Remember, competition might emerge from where you least expect it.

- What are the limits of the organisation in an electronic environment?

- The Internet may change all traditional relations and dependencies; which alliances are (or will be) most profitable for the organisation?

- How can wireless (any place and any time) access to the Internet change the dynamics of the business the organisation is in? What extra values will this provide?

- How does the nature of relations with customers and/or partners change in a virtual value-chain?

- Has the organisation considered sacrificing margins, or even trading in the product, in exchange for a continuous flow of revenues through services? How does this change the business?

- How much does the organisation learn from simply 'doing the business'? With the right measures in the right places any transaction or interaction can become a learning opportunity. Does the organisation become 'smarter' every day? (Partly derived from Centres for IBM e-business Innovation 2000).

The following section contains a description of the contents of this book, and guidelines for various groups of readers.

THE CONTENTS OF THIS BOOK

This book was first and foremost written for managers. It also has an academic perspective. This means that – depending on your interests – you may choose to read only parts of the book.

In Chapter 2 the concept of business models is elaborated and the theory behind them is discussed in a general framework. This chapter has an academic undertone. Chapter 3 describes the presuppositions of the book. It presents a value model, which forms the basis for the typology of business models. The main lines of this typology are discussed. For managers it is important to read this chapter, because it may help you identify which of the remaining chapters are most relevant to your needs.

TIP FOR MANAGERS

If you are pressed for time, just focus on parts of the book. Chapter 2 consists of a literary review and can be skipped, if such things are of no interest to you. Once you have read Chapter 3 you can decide for yourself which of the Chapters 4, 5 and 6, are applicable to your situation.

The three types of business models we distinguish will be discussed in Chapters 4, 5, and 6, successively. In Chapter 4 the Chameleon model is presented. In this business model, efficiency and customer orientation take a central place. Chapter 5 addresses the Innovator model. As the name implies this business model is aimed specifically at the creation of new products or services (innovation). Chapter 6 presents the Foyer model. This business model emphasises the growing importance of communication between people, the consequences of the emotion – and the experience – economy for organisations. Chapter 7 illustrates the dynamics of business models. In reality, the three types are rarely found in pure form. After all, organisations seldom choose a single way of doing business, but rather a combination of models. In some cases organisations are moving from one type of business model to another, and display elements of both. Aside from a discussion of the dynamics in this chapter, three experts voice their opinion on the three types, and on the motivations for a choice of a business model in practice.

CONCLUSIONS

The focus on business models raises a number of questions. Are we really witnessing a new phenomenon? We sympathise with the opinion that not everything in our explanation of a business model is completely new or untried. However, this does not mean that nothing new is happening here. The enormous opportunities of the Internet combined with the many IT applications that have already been developed or are especially designed for this purpose, lead to new intelligent combinations with existing business concepts. This book describes three types of business model that are in keeping with the trends presented in this first chapter. Individualisation, knowledge sharing, innovation and the search for involvement and authenticity are developments that should be taken very seriously by organisations. We are well aware of how difficult it is for managers and others to make informed decisions about these aspects of business. The uncertainty about the outcome of these developments is significant. Because organisations must opt for drastic change at a time when traditional business models are still effective, the decision is made even harder. Nevertheless, most organisations cannot escape the question: What should our next business model be?

CHAPTER 2

What is a Business Model?

'Business model' was one of the buzz words of the Internet Boom. An organisation did not need a strategy, a special competence or even any customers – all it needed was a web-based business model that promised great profits in some vague, distant future. That time has passed and business models have been taken seriously for over a decade, but there is still much confusion about what business models are and how they can be used. Although authors have offered various definitions of 'business model', none appear to be generally accepted. This lack of consensus may, in part, be attributed to interest in the concept from a wide range of disciplines, all of which have found a connection to the term. To better understand business models, this chapter reviews the literature and identifies and classifies the components of business models cited therein. It becomes clear that the concept of business models has been described in various ways, such as the manner of revenue generation, the structure of the organisation, the core competence of the organisation or the way of creating value through the Internet. We have also found that countless combinations of business models are not only possible, but applied in practice. However, there is no single dominant model. A consensus seems to be emerging that business model innovation may be more important than any other source of new venture success.

Adoption of a Technology

A considerable delay – several decades, usually – lies between the technologies that set a revolution in motion and the revolution's heyday. If a powerful new technology appears, it might take people a decade to hear about it and try it. But three decades? Five decades? That something else, I believe, is that many arrangements, many improvements and many organizational changes need to be put in place before the new technology cluster can become widespread. It is not enough that the base technologies of a revolution become available. Whether these are railroads or microchips, a revolution doesn't fully arrive until we structure our activities – our organizations and business methods – around its technologies, and until these technologies adapt themselves to us by becoming comfortable and easy to use. So it's not merely that the base technologies have to become better, faster, cheaper. That

> helps, but what's needed for the revolution to fully blossom are the 1,001 subtechnologies, arrangements, and architectures that adapt us to the new technologies and them to us. Their arrival takes time, and it defines the buildout period as one that creates the arrangements and subtechnologies that bring the new possibilities into full use.
>
> (Arthur 2002)

INTRODUCTION

This chapter focuses on the theories about business models that have appeared. The concept of business models is used in many fields including traditional strategy theory, general management, innovation and information management literature and the emergent body of literature on e-business. As a result, business model concepts contain different source ideas and assumptions and the amount of attention differs widely between them. Some have an organisation-centric view, others focus on value constellations. Some concentrate on strategy, others on operational aspects. Some authors pay particular attention to (information) technology, others to innovation.

The evolution of business model research can be divided into five phases (Gordijn et al. 2005). When the term business model began to become prominent, a number of authors suggested business model definitions and classifications (Applegate 2001; Timmers 1998; Rappa 2003). Taxonomies enumerate a finite number of business model types. In the second phase, authors started to complete the definitions by proposing which elements belonged in a business model. At first, these propositions were simple shopping lists, merely mentioning the components of a business model (Chesbrough and Rosenbloom 2002; Magretta 2002). It was only in the third phase that detailed descriptions of these components followed (Weill and Vitale 2001).

In the fourth phase, researchers began to model the components conceptually. Authors tried to explain that a business model consists of related building blocks or components, allowing the description of an infinite number of business models. During this phase, models were also more rigorously evaluated. Finally, in the ongoing fifth phase, the models are being put into practice in organisations.

In this chapter we will not discuss all the ideas and thoughts that have been pronounced on the term business model, on the contrary, we have tried to identify the mainstream ideas. Despite differences, it appears that there

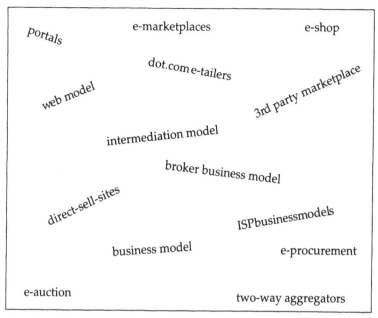

Figure 2.1   Ratatouille of terms

are indeed similarities between the various accounts of business models. It is possible to make a global classification along the following two categories:

- The revenue model, which refers to the specific manner in which an organisation/network is able to generate income.

- The integrated model, which refers to the strategy and the configuration of the organisation and/or the network, designed to exploit business opportunities.

THE REVENUE MODEL

When the term 'business model' became fashionable for Internet-based businesses, it was generally applied to the description of the underlying financial flows, the revenues and the costs that were inherent to the business. Nowadays, this is referred to as the revenue model. The revenue model lays out the process by which an organisation actually makes money by specifying how it is going to charge (or subsidise in the case of advertising supported models) for the services provided. The business model lays out the strategy – what should be done, and how, to create value. The revenue model lays out the execution – how to convert the value creation into cash-flow. Strategy revolves around the determination of the overall vision, the strategic goals and the values you wish to provide. Revenue models revolve around the manner in which the potential of the Internet, e-business, and e-commerce is incorporated in a new and creative way. Thus, they do not focus on the basic technology, hard- or software, but mainly on the new business concepts that become possible.

REVENUES, CORE COMPETENCES AND THE RESOURCE BASED VIEW

> *"A revenue model refers to the specific modes in which a business model enables revenue generation" (Amit and Zott 2000).*

When it was discovered that profits could be made on the Internet in both traditional and utterly new ways, an abundance of articles emerged. A number of authors provided overviews of the methods for revenue generation on the Internet: such as the sales of subscriptions, advertising revenues and transaction revenues (transaction revenues consist of fixed transaction costs, referral costs and variable or fixed sales commissions (Amit and Zott 2000)). According to these authors, organisations can choose a business model on the basis of one of these methods. This interpretation is clearly limited, since it addresses only the ways of 'making money'.

Rappa (2000) also defines a business model as 'the method of doing business by which a organisation can sustain itself' and notes that the business model is clear about how an organisation generates revenues and where it is positioned in the value chain. Rappa presents a taxonomy of business models observed on the web, currently listing nine categories.

In practice these models are often used in combination.

Taxonomy of Web Business Models (Rappa, 2000)

- Brokerage
- Advertising
- Infomediary
- Merchant
- Manufacturer
- Affiliate
- Community
- Subscription
- Utility

Green (1999) goes one step further and approaches a business model from the viewpoint of the core competence or the core skills of the organisation. The core competence consists of the thing the organisation is really good at and by which it distinguishes itself from other organisations. Based on the analysis of the core competences the organisation may arrive at a revenue model. Along the same lines, but from a broader perspective, other authors look at the way core competences as well as other organisational tools, such as a good IT infrastructure, can be employed for value creation. This is referred to as the 'resource based view' of organisations (Wernerfelt 1984; Barney 1991; Peteraf 1993, Amit and Schoemaker 1993).

THE INTEGRATED BUSINESS MODEL

The revenue model, of which a few examples were provided in the previous section, is part of the strategic question of how to position a business. None of the aforementioned authors addresses the question: 'How does an organisation facilitate transactions that create values for all participants, including partners, suppliers and customers?'

> In class, for example, Harvard Business School Professor Applegate said that she forbids students from replying to a question like "What is your business model?" with a statement as simplistic as "A B2B portal." Instead, students must supply answers about what was, and remains, vital in business: customers, products, value propositions, the capabilities and advantages any player brings that will allow the plans to meet success (Lagace 2000)

Authors who have approached business models from the perspective of the strategy and the design of the organisation/network, have tried to answer this question. The strategic choice of organisations remains the starting point of the business model in the literature, but this choice is combined with the design of the organisation and/or the network, the so-called integrated business model. Before we discuss the literature on the design of the business, we will first address the role of strategy and IT in business models.

STRATEGY AND IT

One of the pre-eminent authors in the area of the role of strategy in business models is Porter (2001). He feels that, despite the new opportunities afforded by IT, his classical competitive model for strategy is also still applicable to the development of new business models. According to him 'virtual' (new) activities will not eliminate physical (traditional) activities. Quite the opposite; since virtual activities and physical activities complement each other the relation is strengthened. This notion is based first of all on the fact that IT employment in one activity of the value chain often makes extra demands on physical activities somewhere else in the value chain. Second, unforeseen side effects that arise from IT applications often have to be dealt with through physical activities.

MARKET SPACE

Dutta and Segev (1999) link the term business model to the elements of strategy and IT exclusively. For this they employ the 'market space model'. They propose that in every business model the 'market space' must be defined, to which the organisation wishes to direct its attention. In market space, two dimensions are important: the technological capacity dimension and the strategic business dimension.

The *technological* dimension is built on two important characteristics of the Internet; namely the interactivity and the connectivity. Thanks to the Internet, organisations can now focus on establishing interactive relations with individual customers and on the direct and personal contact with each customer. Because of this the relations grow stronger and new concepts of product design and customer service become possible.

Connectivity entails the creation of a shared global market space, due to the open and global nature of the Internet. This mutual connection leads to the emergence of new communication and coordination mechanisms both between organisations and customers and within groups of organisations and customers themselves.

The *strategic business* dimension of the market space model is based on the classical marketing model of the 4 Ps (Product, Price, Promotion and Placement). One new element takes a central place in the model, namely the 'C' of customer relationship management (CRM).

Figure 2.2 displays the market space model. This model shows how these four Ps and one C are being transformed by the fundamental characteristics of real-time interactivity and global connectivity in the market space of an organisation or network. In this context, the marketing strategy is implicitly regarded as a business model.

IT in the management of the *customer relationship* involves opportunities such as: customer feedback, online customer service, customer identification and customer communities. IT application in *product* concerns, for instance, an online product catalogue, added value information, the online guidance of the

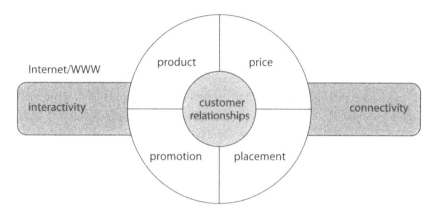

Figure 2.2   Market space model

Source: S. Dutta and A. Segev (1999), Business Transformation on the Internet.

customer, customised products and customer participation in the design of the product. IT opportunities in *promotion* are, for example, the offering of online promotions, customised promotions, and links to other companies, customer participation and online advertising.

IT in *placement* involves, among other things, an online ordering system, real-time processing of orders, online payment system, involvement of partner organisations and online product distribution.

Lastly, IT for the *price* in this market space model covers online price information, demand-based pricing, dynamic composition of prices and customer participation in price determination. According to these authors, the extent to which these elements are present in the business model of an organisation determines, in part, its success. In the market space model, however, a typology of business models remains absent.

VALUE CHAIN

> *The creation of a business model strongly resembles the writing of a new story. To a certain extent of course all new stories are variations to older stories. They are new versions of the universal themes on which human experiences are based. Similarly, all new business models are variations to the general value chain that forms the basis of all businesses (Magretta 2002).*

Ethiraj, Guler and Singh (2000) and Picard (2000) consider the value chain to be the starting point for the business model of an organisation or network. The value chain consists of the various activities that are necessary for the transformation of raw materials into actual products. These are activities like: design, production, marketing, distribution and support activities.

Authors who focus on the value chain usually define value from an economic point of view. The position in the market is determined by the possibilities for the organisation to gain a competitive advantage through the achievement of operational efficiency (cheaper or faster production), or through a change of strategic direction (differentiation), which usually comes down to a customised value chain. This can be achieved through unique products, unique content, unique activities, superior professional knowledge and strong customer- and partner-relations (Porter 2001). Value creation then results in a product or service that meets a market demand (Ethiraj, Guler and Singh 2000).

Michael Dell on Value:

If I understand this correctly, the companies that do nothing but put chips on motherboards don't actually earn tremendous profit doing it. If we want to earn higher returns, shouldn't we be more selective and put our capital into activities where we can add value for our customers, not just into activities that need to get done? I'm not saying those activities are unimportant. They need to get done very, very well. But they're not sources of value that Dell is going to create.

(Magretta 2002)

STRATEGIC NETWORKS

Rappa (2000) approaches the business model from the viewpoint of the position of an organisation in the total value chain, in order to come to a revenue model. This means that a business model is often placed in a network of other companies. This is also acknowledged by Prahalad and Ramaswany (2000) from a strategic perspective. They assert that the object of analysis has moved from one organisation to a network of traditional suppliers, producers, partners, investors and customers. The value chain in this regard is perceived to be much larger than the value chain of one organisation alone. Therefore, in this context one should no longer speak of value chains, but of the *value web*.

Amit and Zott suggest that a business model indicates how transactions are enabled by a network of companies, suppliers, partners and customers.

> *We here define a strategic network as follows: "strategic networks are 'stable' interorganisational ties which are strategically important to participating firms" (Amit and Zott 2000).*

In their business model concept these authors build on the combination of the following theories: the value chain theory of Porter (1985), the strategic network theory of Dyer and Singh (1998) and the transaction costs theory of Williamson (1975). These different theories alone offer only a limited view of the concept of business models, according to Amit and Zott (2000). They examined the value creation potential of a number of American and European e-commerce companies. They developed a model that enables an evaluation of the value creation potential of e-commerce business models along four dimensions: novelty, lock-in, complementarities and efficiency. The value chain theory offers not only a limited view, but is also focused closely on production companies, according to Amit and Zott. Organisations that provide services are much more difficult to place in the model, since information flows are largely omitted. They also view value from more than a financial perspective. Strategic networks, for example, provide access to information, markets and technology. Risk sharing, advantages of economies of scale and range and learning benefits may also be mentioned (see Chapter 5, where the benefits of networks for innovations are described).

NEW RULES!?

Technology changes, economic laws do not (Shapiro and Varian 1999).

An important question that often arises on business models is whether or not new rules come into existence in the new 'global connected knowledge economy', which also lead to new business models (Malhotra 2000). Applegate (2001) states: 'The difference between industrial age business models and e-business models is the different business rules and assumptions about how business is done'. Timmers (1998), however, suggests that for e-business not only are new rules valid, but many old rules are also still applicable. New rules are, for instance, the acknowledgement of the importance of networks, of speed and of the principle 'Let the customer work for you'. Another important new rule is that in value chains and dynamic markets the physical location ('place') is no longer so relevant, but has been overtaken by the combined interaction of relations ('space') (Weill and Vitale 2001).

Aside from these new rules, a number of original rules remain that were inherent to the 'old' economy. These involve customer orientation, market segmentation (and positioning), and being the first on the market. Lastly, trust remains the basis for growth in the mass market.

The concept of business models of Timmers (1998), is based on a combination of new and old principles. His definition has had a great influence on the discussion of this subject. According to him, a business model is:

- an architecture for the products, service and information flows, including a description of the various business activities and the roles of the various participants in the network;

- a description of the potential benefits of the various parties in the network;

- a description of the sources of revenues (Timmers 1998).

In Timmers' view, new business models can be developed by disintegrating the traditional value chains, where individual organisations may concentrate on parts of it. New business models can also emerge through a new combination of different value chains or through new combinations within a traditional value chain.

The new business models are classified on the basis of two criteria, namely the degree of functional integration in the value chain and the degree of innovation. On the basis of this classification, Timmers (1998) distinguishes eleven different types, which are displayed in Figure 2.3.

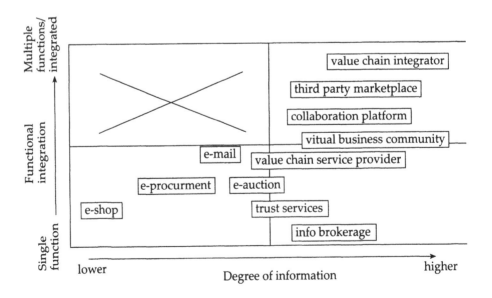

Figure 2.3   Typology of business models

Source: Timmers, P. (1998), Business Models for Electronic Markets, International Journal of Electric Markets

Jansen (2002) also opts for a central strategic perspective, combined with the design perspective, in his model of e-formulas for organisations. From his research he suggests that things often go wrong in the coordination between strategy and design. Starting points in the e-formula are the strategic positioning and the customer. The extent to which the organisation manages to proceed satisfactorily through the various steps in the interaction with the customer determines the success of the organisation or the network. These steps include capturing the customer's interest, tempting the customer to purchase and actually use the product or service, followed by a lock-in of the customer. During all these steps, knowledge about the customer is gathered, to improve the interaction. That is why learning takes a central place in his interaction model.

Weill and Vitale (2001) define an e-business model as a description of the roles and the relations between organisations, customers, partners and suppliers. These authors also believe that a business model must originate from the customer's perspective. Moreover, the focus should be on the sources of revenues and the way these revenues are generated. IT plays an important role in this regard, since this technology facilitates the integration of business processes, workflows, IT infrastructure, knowledge and data. Weill and Vitale describe eight atomic e-business models, each of which can be implemented as a pure e-business model or combined to create a hybrid model.

THE IMPORTANCE OF IT

IT plays a critical role in all business models. Ethiraj, Guler and Singh (2000) examined the changes in opportunity space within firms' value chains arising from online technologies, and its implications for competitive advantage. They identified the following four key components of the business model and discussed how and why these may be important drivers of competitive advantage in Internet-based business models:

- *Scalability*: Information assets, which dominate the e-business world, have a unique property – they are generally costly to produce in the first place, but once produced, very easy (and relatively inexpensive) to reproduce. As a result, first movers in a market have an enormous advantage. They can flood the market, and essentially create a winner-takes-all situation. In order to exploit this aspect of competitive advantage on the web, it follows that companies must develop business models that are scalable.

- *Complementary resources and capabilities*: An organisation with an innovative business model can initially use its technological prowess to steal a march over its competitors. Entrepreneurs would be wrong, however, to believe that this advantage is long-lasting. The web sharply lowers barriers to entry, and rivals can soon catch up with the first mover. In order to protect their competitive positions, companies that lead in the digital arena may have to acquire physical assets to keep their competitors at bay.

- *Relation-specific assets*: No individual firm can hope to dominate the Internet, which is a complex network designed precisely to avoid such dominance. As a result, networks of alliances become increasingly important. Business models on the web must recognise that competitive advantage in e-business is often based on managing collaborative relationships with key partners well.

- *Knowledge-sharing routines*: This condition follows from the previous one, which emphasises the need for strong collaborative relationships. These relationships can only become truly effective if the collaborators develop mechanisms through which they can share knowledge with one another. Such knowledge-sharing will help the partners to enhance their collective competitive advantage over rivals and their partners.

But it is not enough simply to have the characteristics described above. They must actually be employed.

A recently published typology has been developed and studied by Weill et al. (2005). This typology is based on two fundamental dimensions of what a business does. The first dimension – what types of rights are being sold – gives rise to four basic business models: Creator, Distributor, Landlord and Broker. The second dimension – what types of assets are involved – distinguishes between four important asset types: physical, financial, intangible and human. This distinction leads to four subcategories within each of the four basic business models to give a total of sixteen specialised business model types. Of these sixteen possible business models, only seven are common among large companies in the US today. Together, all of these business model types are called the MIT Business Model Archetypes (BMAs) (see Figure 2.4).

REDESIGNING THE BUSINESS MODELS

Only a few authors have devoted their attention to the dynamic aspect of business models. How do you use business models? How do you apply the new design possibilities? Shubar and Lechner (2004) have developed a framework for this, named the IDEA Framework, which functions as an action plan for

Basic business model archetype	What type of asset is involved?			
	Financial	Physical	Intangible	Human
Creator	Entrepreneur	Manufacturer	Inventor	Human creator*
Distributor	Financial trader	Wholesaler/ retailer	IP trader	Human distributor*
Landlord	Financial landlord	Physical landlord	Intellectual landlord	Contractor
Broker	Financial broker	Physical broker	IP broker	HR broker

* These models are illegal in the US and most places today because they involve selling human beings. They are included here for logical completeness.

Figure 2.4   The 16 MIT business model archetypes

Source: P. Weill, T. W. Malone, V. T. D'Urso, G. Herman and S. Woerner (2005) Do Some Business Models Reform Better Than Others? MIT Centre for Coordination, Science Working Paper No. 226

the search for the application of business model thinking. This action plan is illustrated in Figure 2.5.

According to this method, possible business models are evaluated to identify those that have the potential to succeed in the market of the organisation. All considered business models are ranked according to their performance in assumed market scenarios. The aim of this framework is to understand the environment of every single business model that has been identified as well as the dynamics of and the interaction between the business models and thus the dynamics of the industry/market. All identified business models are then placed in the value chain with regard to the value-adding activities they deliver to this environment (Shubar and Lechner 2004). In Chapter 7 we will discuss several aspects of the dynamics of business models.

BUSINESS MODELS IN PRACTICE

The application of business models is typically a history of sector-wide management fads and investment waves (see the dot-com boom). In spite of all the talk about business models, there have been very few large-scale systematic empirical studies of them. Weill et al. (2005) state that we do not even know, for instance, how common the different kinds of business models are and whether some business models will perform better financially than others. Using the framework in Figure 2.4, these authors have classified the revenue streams

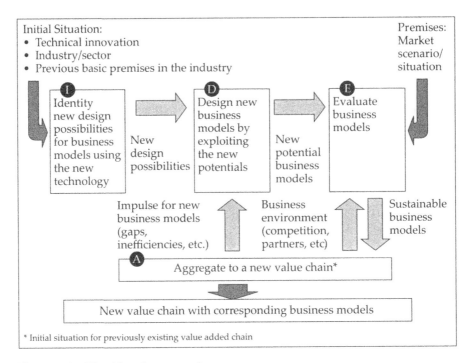

Figure 2.5   The idea framework

Source: A. Shubar, U. Lechner (2004) The Public WLAN Market and Its Business Models. 17th Bled e-Commerce Conference 2004

of the top 1000 firms in the US economy in the fiscal year 2000 and analysed their financial performance. The results show that business models are a better predictor of financial performance than industry classifications and that for at least two broad measures of financial performance – profit and market value – some business models do, indeed, perform better than others. Specifically, selling the right to use assets is more profitable and more highly valued by the market than selling ownership of assets.

It is clear that further empirical research on business models is needed. However, the first results of this study by Weill and colleagues afford a promising insight into the potential success of the business model concept.

DEFINITION OF A BUSINESS MODEL

Based on the current ideas and concepts, we have opted for a typology of business models in this book based on four components essential to each business model. The starting point is the strategy of the organisation or the network. In the formulation of this strategy, statements must be made about the value model. A value model consists of the values that are created for all participants, including partners, suppliers and customers. To create these values, a cohesive whole is needed, consisting of the following elements, which are tuned in to each other: strategy, processes, IT and governance. For this reason we have chosen the following definition of the term business model:

> *A business model is a unique configuration of elements that consist of the strategy, processes, technologies, and the governance of the organisation. This configuration is formed to create value for the customers and thus to compete successfully in a particular market (in part drawn from Ethiraj, Guler and Singh 2000).*

In Figure 2.6 these elements of the definition and their mutual relations are displayed.

These elements will be developed and elaborated on per type of business model in the following chapters.

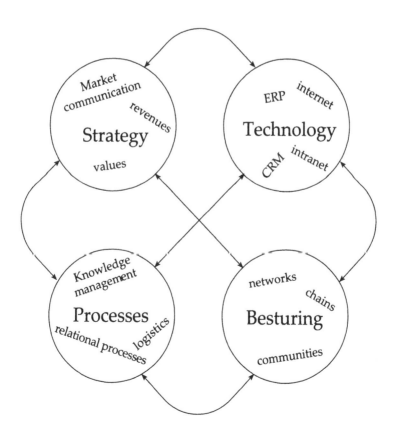

Figure 2.6 Elements of definition business model

CONCLUSIONS

The fact that such a substantial body of literature has been published on the subject of business models is a clear sign of the significance that is attributed to the concept. A good business model, after all, lights the path for the organisation or the network (the strategy) and directs how one employs the strategy (design). Moreover, a business model is an important tool for the communication with customers, employees and partners. Because a business model 'tells a good story', it has the crucial function of aligning the ideas of everyone in and around the organisation concerning the values the organisation (or network) wants to create (Magretta 2002).

However, the question remains whether or not managers, who want to tell this 'good story', will benefit much from the models and theories that have been developed so far. A review of the literature makes it clear, for instance, that there is no single generally accepted definition of the term business model. Neither can one find a generally accepted taxonomy of business models. Nonetheless, despite this diversity of ideas we do see some similarities. Presently the general conception is that a business model involves more than just the manner of revenue generation. The importance of the design of the internal organisation and of the network the organisation operates in; the relationship with the customers and the strategic role of IT is emphasised in most research articles and books on business models. Also, the consensus seems to be emerging that business model innovation may be more important than any other source of new venture success.

In this chapter we have tried to identify some trends in the vast body of literature. In this book we have opted for the integrated business model. This means that an organisation (or network) must choose a business model in which the strategic choice for the value model, the design of organisation and IT are described. In the following chapter this value model and the typology of business models on which it is based are discussed.

CHAPTER 3

Innovation, Customisation and Authenticity

In providing their products and services, organisations or networks offer all kinds of value to the customer. Depending on the customer's appreciation of these values, the organisation or network will be more or less successful. But providing value involves more than one-way traffic. Managers should carefully consider the reciprocal value that is expected from the customer in return for the provided products or services. One of the common reciprocal values obviously is monetary, but information and communication technology offers organisations the possibility of receiving several different, very interesting values from the customer, such as customer profiles or knowledge.

INTRODUCTION

This chapter presents the value model that forms the starting point for the business models in this book. A value model is a certain combination of values

What is interesting about the railway revolution in Great Britain, is that the crash of 1847 was by no means the end of the railway. The major buildout of railways came after the crash. After 1847, rail transportation did not only become better, faster, and cheaper with improvements such as steel rails and compound locomotives. The most important innovations involved new technology, such as lever systems that worked with signals and switches, traffic control via telegraph, air brakes, sleeping trains, dining cars and toilets on trains. (Toilets arrives later on English trains than on American trains due to a certain English indisposition to admit bodily functions in public.) In the expansion phase a new technology is continuously adapted to human use. And business in turn adapts itself to the railway. In every important revolution, business organisation needs to do more than adapt. It needs to some considerable degree redefine and redesign themselves. This held true for previous technological revolutions, but it remains so for the present adaptation to IT and the Internet. The problem is that organisations do not yet know how to restructure themselves and their activities. (Arthur 2002) provided *to* a customer, and reciprocal values, received *from* a customer. In this chapter we suggest that not every combination of values will lead to an effective business model, but that logical combinations reveal three ideal types of business models. In the following section, four assumptions are discussed that lie at the core of the business models in this book. The most important elements from the business models will be explained later. The three types of business model, the Chameleon, the Innovator and the Foyer, are introduced.

BASIC ASSUMPTIONS

This book presents a value model based on four essential assumptions.

- The functioning of all organisations (and networks of organisations) ensures that certain values are provided to various parties. These might involve consumers of products or services, employees, stockholders, but society in general as well. The first and most important assumption in this book is that in the question of value determination, the focus should be on the receiving party (customer).

- The second assumption is that the way governance is organised in the relationship between customer and organisation, together with the chosen combination of values, forms the foundation for a classification of types. Since business models are considered from the design perspective in this book, governance is an important issue. As described in Chapter 1, the design approach describes the way in which activities in an organisation or network are organised in structures. Structures in which the division of labour, but particularly the governance, are arranged and formalised.

- The third assumption is that the choice for a combination of values and the manner of governance determines the way the organisation organises its processes, determines its organisation culture and presents itself to the outside world. This makes the chosen value model decisive for the degree of success that can be realised.

- The fourth assumption is that the choice for a value model should never exclude other values. The decision on which values and reciprocal values deserve the focus of the organisation is made at a particular time due to, for example, the circumstances that apply. But this choice should be evaluated periodically and other values should be considered. This assumption emphasises the dynamic character of the typology in this book. The choice for a certain type of business model always involves the search for balance between the components that are part of it.

The following sections in this chapter provide further foundations of, and elaborate on, these assumptions.

STRATEGY OF A BUSINESS MODEL

As suggested in the previous section, the first step towards a new business model involves the choice of values the organisation (or the network) wants to create for the customer and the values the organisation or the network wishes to receive as compensation for these values. Value is traditionally defined as the meaning (monetary or otherwise) that can be assigned to a possession or asset.

To make the concept of value more clear, a distinction was made between the values for the organisation and the values for the customer. From here on we assume the following definitions for value and reciprocal value.

> **Value** is the result offered to the customer of the activities of the organisation (network) performs.
>
> **Reciprocal value** is the result of the process the customer offers to engage in as compensation for what is received from the organisation (network).

The choice for the combination of values and reciprocal values and the choice for a physical or digital implementation of the same, is referred to as the *value model* in this book. Important elements in this value model include the focus on the customer, the combination of the values and the fact that IT enables the offering of new values. The choice of strategy for generating revenues, the revenue model, is merely a part of the value model.

CUSTOMER FOCUS

The concept of value has over time enjoyed various interpretations and differing degrees of attention. In profit organisations the term *stockholder value* was introduced in the 1970s. The goal of a business became the creation of value; investments were judged by their ability to add value to the organisation. The emphasis on stockholder value has had the effect, amongst other things, of creating a climate in business of business-like and efficiency driven behaviour. This has often led to a neglect of many organisational aspects, since all other interests of the organisation were deemed inferior to it. It even led to disrupted relations with and between employees and customers.

A well-known historical example was the reaction to the profit results of the multinational organisation Shell. At the time, there was a profit increase of 12 per cent. Management then felt that, for the sake of the stockholders, this result should be raised to 14 per cent. This led to a process of reorganisation with large personnel reductions. The employees and trade unions had a difficult time understanding this decision and the reorganisation led to all kinds of problems.

The question that has arisen since the 1990s is that of the legitimacy and continuity of organisations. This question stems from a strategic perspective that considers values over the *long term* as opposed to the short term, where the emphasis seems to be on increasingly higher stock exchange indices.

The approach in this book also features the question of value creation, both for stockholders and for other stakeholders as well. Slowly, the approach that focuses on the customer as the pivotal stakeholder is gaining ground, the so-called *customer perspective*. Organisations should attempt to pinpoint the unique value(s) that only they can offer. Increasingly important in this regard is the question of what values the customers can offer the organisation as 'reciprocal payment'. It goes without saying that the stockholders benefit from this exchange if it leads to success for the organisation/network.

VALUES

Theories by Porter (1985) and Treacy and Wiersema (1995), among others, state that organisations must make a clear decision when it comes to choosing the values they want to provide. Porter makes the point that organisations cannot excel in everything. Treacy and Wiersema also suggest that no single organisation today can achieve success by trying to please the customer on all fronts. An organisation may choose to offer a lower consumer's price, and thereby achieve competitive advantage, by implementing and continuously improving highly efficient business processes. However, this often means that the provided products and/or services do not, to a greater or lesser extent, meet individual customers' needs. This is the choice for 'operational excellence'. On the other hand, organisations may prefer a strategy of 'customer intimacy' which entails the adaptation of products and services to the requirements of specific customers. Usually, meeting specific customers' demands involves a trade-off with efficiency. However, the customers may, in these cases, accept a higher price, since their personal expectations are met. The third strategy is the so-called 'product leadership' strategy. An organisation following a product leadership strategy attempts to present itself as the most prominent and innovative organisation in the business of a certain type of product or service. Figure 3.1 illustrates these three strategies.

In practice however, successful organisations or networks offer combinations of values. In a study on 1500 'e-entrepreneurs' Jansen found that approximately half of the studied organisations not only opted for a combination of three or more values, but indeed were capable of maintaining this general excellence (Jansen 2002). Thanks to the ability of IT to offer personalised value to customers, to improve quality and further efficiency, organisations and networks can direct their attention to a greater range of values than previously. Moreover, a number of these values then go on to lead to new unforeseen values.

NEW VALUES

When it comes to providing new values, increasingly it is values in the form of the delivery of extra services created especially for the customer, that come to the fore.

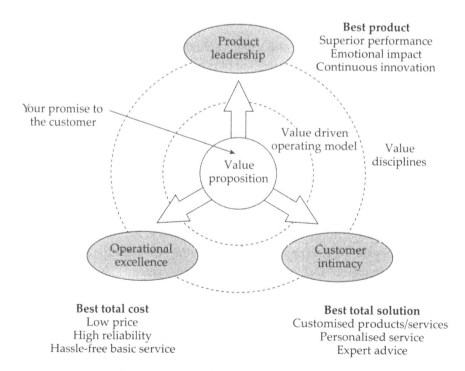

Figure 3.1   Strategies based on values

Source: Treacy, M. and Wiersma, F. (1995), The Discipline of Market Leaders, New York, HarperCollins Publishers.

Table 3.1   Values

Values
• products and services
• authenticity
• something 'new'
• quality on demand
• feeling of belonging
• participation

Thus, in practice, organisations offer new values to customers. These stem in part from customers' desire for other values, such as authenticity and experience. But customers increasingly demand, aside from new values, (innovation) combinations of values. Sometimes an organisation can indeed deliver such a combination, but in many cases the result of this customer demand is that cooperation is required, in the form of various networks.

The Value of Microsoft and the Network

'A key reason for Microsoft's enormous added value is the existence of the Intel Corporation and the complementarity between both organisations' products'

(Brandenburger and Nalebuff 1997)

RECIPROCAL VALUES

Aside from the value(s) that the organisation offers its customer, there is today a growing interest in the value that the customer may offer to the organisation. This involves mainly the addition value the customer can provide above the monetary value, in the form of – for example – information and knowledge. Here IT plays an important role, since IT makes it possible for organisations to harvest and process this customer information and knowledge.

At the same time, an increasing differentiation of reciprocal values can be observed in practice. In this manner, customers can generate ideas for product development, provide information that can lead to customer profiles and aid in the design and realisation of products/services.

Table 3.2   Reciprocal values

Reciprocal values
• money
• information
• loyalty
• relations
• ideas
• co-creation

VALUE CREATION IN BRICKS AND CLICKS

These days, values and reciprocal values are no longer created solely in the physical world (also referred to as the world of 'bricks'), but also in the electronic or virtual world (the world of 'clicks') (Gulati and Garino 2000). In the process of selecting an effective business model, it is first and foremost important to reflect on which values and which reciprocal values one wishes to offer and receive. Subsequently one must consider in which way these (reciprocal) values might take shape, in the electronic world, the physical world, or both. In this context, it is important to focus on the co-ordination between both worlds.

To render the concepts of both values and reciprocal values less abstract, in Figure 3.2, two arrows each represent a process of value adding in one of these worlds. Figure 3.2 has been filled in by means of an example, namely the Internet organisation Amazon.com. Many technological firms involve their customers in the innovation process, receiving customers' ideas as reciprocal value. In Chapter 5 we will discuss this in more detail.

The value adding for both customer and organisation/network is at the core of our typology. As suggested, the choice for the value model is an important part of the strategy of a business model. Another important element in each business model is the question of governance. This subject is discussed in the following section.

GOVERNANCE IN A BUSINESS MODEL

Approaching business models from a design perspective entails focusing attention on one of the most important aspects of design, namely the way in which the governance of the organisation or network is arranged.

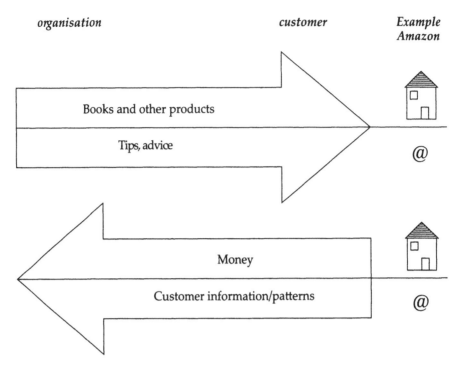

Figure 3.2   Value model applied to Amazon.com

THREE FORMS OF GOVERNANCE

In this book we make a distinction between three basic forms of governance. In the first form, control is completely in the hands of a (central) organisation. The organisation determines the strategy, and coordinates and executes the business processes. The customer only features as a consumer of the provided products/services and as a supplier of money and, for example, customer information. In the second form of governance, the organisation has yielded part of the direction and control to the customer, but also to co-producers and/ or suppliers. This may occur when the organisation is no longer in possession of the total knowledge to produce the required products or services. Together, the organisation, partners and customers engage in the development process and together they define (at least in part) the design of their co-operation. The third form of governance has been on the rise since the early days of the Internet. In it, the customer determines the strategy and the business processes (as far as one can speak of them as such). In each of these forms of governance, different values are exchanged between either customer–organisation or customer–customer. In the subsequent section three types of business model are described, each involving a different value model and one of the three forms of governance.

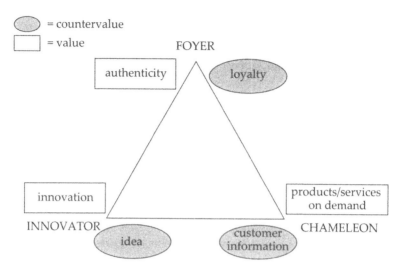

Figure 3.3   Typology of business models

TYPOLOGY OF BUSINESS MODELS

In Chapter 1 we described three new values as reactions to developments in the
organisational environment. These are the values of customisation, innovation
and authenticity. The developments in value-adding reveal a trend over time.
Delivering products and services that are personalised to the customers' demand
has been a strategic choice for a growing number of organisations for about two
decades. Innovation has obviously been present in the form of inventions since
the onset of human creativity. The business model in our typology that focuses
on innovation, however, revolves not around isolated inventions, but rather
around the process of their exploitation in the form of collaborative knowledge
sharing efforts, facilitated by IT and the Internet. Innovative collaboration
between various parties has occurred increasingly in the past decade, in the
form of alliances and virtual organisations. In recent years much attention
has been given both in organisations and in professional literature to the
need for involvement, authenticity and emotion. The satisfying of these needs
takes various forms, but is particularly represented in all kinds of (Internet)
communities. The need for meaningful interaction with each other has always
been part of human nature. The growing individualisation, commercialisation
and higher educational levels of Western society on the one hand, and the
potential of the Internet to fulfil this need by means of virtual communities on
the other encourage a growing attention to emotion and involvement. Figure
3.3 shows the typology of the three business models that have been categorised
on the basis of their value models and the forms of governance.

This typology consists of three types of business models, each of which represents a dominant value of the organisation to the customer, and a value of the customer to the organisation. Each type of business model is characterised by its own form of governance.

CHAMELEON

The first type of business model we call *Chameleon*. Organisations that choose the Chameleon model will always need to provide a (unique) added value, in order to achieve competitive advantage (Dörflinger and Marxt 2001). This added value springs from the combination of customisation and efficiency. Punctuality, fast service and convenience are also values in this type that are important to the customer. The business model is called *Chameleon* because it describes a form of organisation that does not change its core features, yet adapts its appearance to conform to the demands of the environment/customer.

The combination of customisation and efficiency of the Chameleon organisation ensures that the customer cannot realise the same added value in any other way. Thus customer commitment is the result of a unique combination of product and service qualities. An organisation can only achieve this unique added value if it obtains information from a customer. The organisation receives as reciprocal value the customer's personal information, on the basis of which customer profiles and purchase patterns can be established. Therein lies the mutual dependence.

The Chameleon mode, among all three types, is the one most oriented towards the (business) interests of the organisation. The organisation fulfils a central role and is in (near) complete control. The customer is given a few selected options, and the building of a real and authentic personal relationship with the customer is not part of the model. The customer relation is therefore only a business relationship, directed solely towards the establishment of a transaction.

INNOVATOR

The second type of business model is the *Innovator*. The value this type of business model offers to the customer lies in the new, the advanced, and thereby the feeling of 'being ahead'. In exchange for products and services, customers provide the organisation (network) with ideas on new products and/or services; they collaborate with the organisation about developments and opportunities and about the expansion and application of innovations. The term 'Innovator' indicates what this business model is really about.

Clothing

Buying clothes on the Internet doesn't seem too difficult. You know your own size and it's easy to choose your clothes on a website. In practice, people have not only different sizes, but also different haircolour, different colour of their eyes and also the shape of people's body is completely different. Lands End sells clothing on the Internet. They have a traditional catalogue and of course they keep the information of customers' sizes and buying patterns. But there is more to make their customers feel confident. You can build your own virtual model. "With the My Virtual Model™ feature, you can try Lands End clothing on a model that's practically a mirror image of yourself. Business suits to bathrobes, let your model try it on before you buy. All without even setting foot in a dressing room."

The Innovator differs from the *traditional* innovative organisation, where inventions were made by 'Gyro Gearloose's' in their own garages, or in isolated Research & Development laboratories. In the Innovator organisation, inventions are commercially exploited in a network, consisting of, amongst others, organisations, customers and suppliers. The relationship between the network and the customer is radically different from that in the Chameleon, since customers are part of the Innovator model. This is a model of shared governance.

Furthermore, who the customer is, is not set in stone, since in certain situations the supplier can become the customer and the customer, for example, a supplier. In order to make inventions commercially applicable, knowledge sharing is of paramount importance. Knowledge management is thus an important process in the Innovator model.

Innovation emphasises long term effectiveness as opposed to the more short term efficiency of, for example, the Chameleon business model. The Innovator predicates a structural capacity within the organisation to innovate. This is a much broader concept than simply a technological competence. It involves the design of the organisation and its network, (knowledge) management, and the potential for communication of its IT facilities and so on.

FOYER

The third type of business model that is identified in our typology is the *Foyer* model. In this business model type, real personal relations exist between the participants. The value the organisation offers the participant includes a feeling

---

Networking for Competitive Edge

VTT Technical Research Centre of Finland is the largest technological research and development organisation in the Nordic region. With a number of unique research facilities, covering everything from electronics to construction, and heavily involved in many EU projects and national innovation networks, VTT wants to help its customers see beyond the businesses they have now, to the businesses they could have in the future, and help them introduce new solutions to achieve their potential. VTT believes that partnerships are the best means for transferring and leveraging knowledge and technology. Therefore VTT gives much attention to customer focus and cooperation with other innovators, as part of the organisation's efforts to improve the global competitiveness of its customers by creating and applying new technology.

Working together with a group of specialist aluminium, plastic, sheet metal and electrical component companies, VTT has developed a new networking model for providing customers with rapid and easy access to information on new materials and technical solutions. The network makes it possible for customers, suppliers and manufacturers to study alternatives for producing new, competitive end-products and select the best and fastest ones that suit their needs.

(www.hightechfinland.com/2006/hightech_country/en_GB/vtt/)

---

of shared identity, of belonging and being part of a group. The most extreme form of the Foyer mode involves complete authenticity, meaning that the organisation does not act out of ulterior motives. For instance, a marketing plan may create an illusion of a shared identity with the customer. Customers have a sense of wanting to reconnect with a value system that is deeper than what's on sale. In the Foyer organisation, a genuine community with its own shared identity exists. The customer offers their loyalty in return for the authentic values received. We have chosen the name *Foyer* for this model, since this term represents values associated with the hearth, a source of warmth and light.

The Foyer organisation is very open; the participants are the decisive factor and they control what happens. Governance therefore, is in the hands of the participants themselves. The social interaction between the participants is supported and facilitated by IT, which simultaneously constitutes the platform on which the relationships and communities originate.

Terra Madre

Terra Madre was founded in 2004 as a result of a meeting of people in the food business. During this meeting 5000 small farmers, fishermen and food producers from all over the world discussed their daily life problems. They especially wanted to exchange knowledge of each others solutions, experiences and ideas. This network has developed into a virtual global community, where information and experiences are shared. Real life meetings are the result: cheese producers from a certain region visited colleagues in other parts of the world both to learn and to help with set up of the business or quality improvement of the cheese products.

CONCLUSIONS

The typology presented in this chapter, with its underlying value model and forms of governance, offers an addition to current theories on business models, since it explicitly reveals the (reciprocal) values and value exchanges between participants. This approach differs from the way business models are usually discussed in the literature. In existing models, it is mainly the hard values (products, services and money) that form the centre of discussion. The focus is rarely on the softer values, such as information, experience, authenticity, trust and identity, if they are considered at all. Consequently, new organisational forms, such as virtual communities, cannot be explained, or are difficult to classify.

This typology features multiple values and reciprocal values. It is by the combination of these values that organisations may discover opportunities to arrive at new business models. The value model and this typology can thus serve as a starting point for a dialogue within the organisation and its networks.

CHAPTER 4

The Chameleon Model

For some time now organisations have been faced with two developments. The first of these is growing individualisation. This has led to a drastic increase in the demand for services that are tailored to match the demands and circumstances of an individual customer. Second, the capacity for doing business that is focused on individual customers has increased sharply due to developments in information- and communication-technology. The satisfaction of individual customers' needs is one of the most important current trends that determine the success of certain products or services. It is for this reason that organisations attempt to generate customer-specific information, in order to be able to offer (modular) personalised products and services. The business model that integrates these two developments is the Chameleon.

Hilton Hotels: a new definition of service

Hilton Hotels Corp. aims to raise customer service to a level previously impossible for an Internet business, claims Bruce Rosenberg, vice-president of Market Distribution. The online booking system provides hotel information and virtual tours through Hilton hotels all over the world. Regular guests can sign up on this website for the free HHONORS bonus program and benefit in various ways. One of the bonuses of this program is a service that is automatically customised on the basis of preferences recorded in previous visits to the Hilton. 'When we first introduced the concept of a website in a presentation to management, it was met with both support and a great extent of scepticism. Just having a website is not enough in our business environment; there must be clear goals and a "return on investment",' says Rosenberg. 'A website must be implemented properly and that is why we have to change our complete business model. What we were doing yesterday won't work anymore. Hilton wants a larger percentage of the travellers' business, 35 percent to 50 percent.' says Rosenberg. 'This means that Hilton must elevate both the service and the experience customers have with us to an unprecedented level. The Internet has opened eyes on how we can and ought to do business. We have looked at all business models – every customer segment from the traveller on business, the tourist, the organiser of meetings, to travel agencies – and we have identified the electronic ways of doing business with these segments.' This involves information, interactivity, the functionality of booking and personalisation. 'We want profiles of the customers, their history with us, what they do and don't like. Hilton already has components of a "totally integrated customer environment," with excellent profiles of the most frequent guests: the members of HHONORS. But the information on guests that stay only occasionally at the Hilton is less elaborate and these guests number in the tens of millions per year. It is this group that offers great opportunities for growth. Through the Internet we can approach them more efficiently and build a deeper personal relationship to them', says Rosenberg. 'We could not do this before by approaching them through the mail. This would have greatly exceeded our budget.' The new business model for Hilton is, however, a costly venture in itself. The website alone has costs running into 'seven figures every year'. Receiving more business from each customer requires meeting each customer's specific demands concerning hotel rooms (location, size of the bed, Internet services, etc.), but also concerning food and other matters, which is complex and expensive to arrange. 'Finding a balance between the costs and benefits of such levels of service, is an important issue. To be able to handle this complexity, we enhanced the training and knowledge level of our employees.' The motivation for doing this is there, since Hilton's website has already delivered positive results. 'We know how many guests have visited our website (millions every month) and the revenues they generate,' says Rosenberg. 'Whichever way you analyse it, we are seeing a positive return on investment!'

INTRODUCTION

The Chameleon is an animal that is known for its ability to adapt to its environment. The business model described in this chapter is called Chameleon (see Figure 4.1), because it describes an organisational form that does not change at its core, but adapts its appearance in response to the demands of the customer. After all, only the colours of the Chameleon change when the animal finds itself in a different environment.

The strategy of the Chameleon is discussed in the next section. In this first section we explore the balance between personalisation and efficiency. Subsequent sections present the values that are provided to the customer and the reciprocal values the customer offers the organisation and also focuses on the design of the Chameleon organisation. This includes the design principles and the processes that characterise this business model. Central to the design

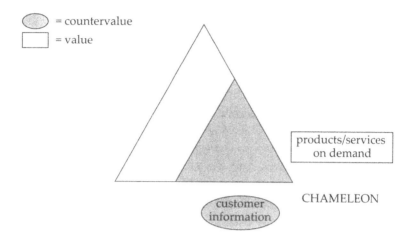

Figure 4.1   Business model Chameleon

are customer-relationship management, the design of the logistic process and the demands that these make on IT applications like ERP (Enterprise Resource Planning) and CRM (Customer Relationship Management).

STRATEGY

To obtain competitive advantage, organisations will always need to provide a unique added value (Dörflinger and Marxt 2001). This involves a strategic choice. An organisation may choose to focus on cost reduction. This choice may lead in turn to a lower price for the consumer and thus to a competitive advantage for the organisation. However, a product or service offering based solely on price may often mean that the delivered products and/or services only partially meet the demands of individual customers. In Chapter 3 this strategy was referred to as 'operational excellence' (Treacy and Wiersema 1995).

On the other hand, organisations may prefer to make customer requirements central to their strategy. In this case, customers may accept a higher price, since it enables their personal wishes to be met accurately. The strategy that accompanies the Chameleon business model is not simply a choice for an individual customer, but a combination of two strategic choices:

- personalisation: the matching of products/services to the personal wishes and/or needs of the customer;

- efficiency: making the production of products/services as cost-effective as possible.

The key here is to find the right balance.

VALUE MODEL

The value model, as described in Chapter 3, is the starting point for the various types of business models. An important value the Chameleon offers its customers is *personalisation*, meaning a repertoire of products and services that is adapted to the customers' demands. The combination of personalisation and efficiency in the Chameleon is accomplished through a modular organisation of products and/or services, and the provision of a specific combination of standard components to each customer. This concept is generally referred to as 'mass customisation' (Gardner 2000). In practice this means that an organisation offers a (limited) number of options to the customer. Which is why, in the Chameleon model, you cannot speak of a 'Customer Intimacy Strategy' (Treacy and Wiersema 1995).

It is the modular set-up of products/services that leads to a differentiated offer. The limited choice-repertoire and the modular set-up enable a large degree of efficiency, so that the accomplishment of two seemingly contradictory goals can be reconciled (Dörflinger and Marxt 2001).

Aside from personalisation, the Chameleon organisation offers customers value in other ways as well, namely saving on selection and purchasing time, convenience and low costs. Because the organisation anticipates the needs of the customer, they can save time otherwise spent searching for the right product/service, the right functionalities or an accurate supplier with attractive pricing. The customer thus saves time and money. The purchase of a product or service is also facilitated (fast service). Both types of values can lead to a more intensive customer lock-in.

The primary reciprocal value for the provision of products/services is monetary. This is discussed in the next section under the revenue model of the Chameleon organisation. In comparison to traditional business models, customers provide the Chameleon with an additional reciprocal value, namely customer information, customer-profiles and purchasing-patterns. This reciprocal value can be obtained because the Chameleon makes use of both the Internet and internal IT-applications, enabling the storage, processing, integration and use of large quantities of customer and production data. Customer data changes over time, because of a changing context. For example interests change, relationships start or end, salaries and social positions change.

Consumers Want Personalisation and Privacy

Personalisation remains something most consumers want, though their privacy fears continue to escalate. According to the second annual personalisation study conducted by personalisation vendor Choicestream, 80 per cent of consumers in the 2005 survey were interested in receiving personalised content.

To get personalised content, 60 per cent of respondents indicated they'd be willing to spend a minimum of two minutes answering questions, up from 56 per cent in 2004. Over a quarter (26 per cent) reported they would be willing to spend at least 6 minutes answering questions, up from 21 per cent last year. Only 12 per cent said they wouldn't be willing to spend any time answering personalisation question, down from 14 per cent in 2004.

Types of content personalisation respondents seek vary with age. Nearly half (47 per cent) of 18 to 24 years olds are more interested in personalised content relating to music. TV and movie content is of interest to 27 per cent, while 24 per cent say they would be interested in receiving personalised content about books. Among the over-50's, news was the top category at 28 per cent, followed by web search (26 per cent) and books (22 per cent). Across all age groups the study finds retailers are leaving 'dollars on the table' because they aren't delivering the personalised content users want and/or need. In particular the study notes 37 per cent of respondents of all ages reported they would have bought more DVDs/videos if they had found more of what they liked. A third (34 per cent) reported a similar mismatch with music.

Despite the fact users want more personalisation and would buy more if they could get more personalised content, they were not willing to share as much personal information as they once were. Respondents indicated decreasing willingness to share preferences (59 per cent in 2005/65 per cent in 2004) and demographic information (46 per cent in 2005/57 per cent in 2004) in exchange for personalised content.

Security of personal data is the biggest personalisation concern. 'The most surprising aspect of the study was the juxtaposition of the interest in personalization versus the fear of personal data loss,' Doug Feick, ChoiceStream's EVP of finance and business affairs told ClickZ Stats. 'Consumers are clearly expressing an interest in a personalised experience. Those same consumers are expressing significant fear about the security of their personal information should they exchange it for a more personalised online experience.'

The study also found only 32 per cent of respondents were willing to allow web sites to track clicks and purchases in exchange for personalised content, down from 41 per cent in 2004. Feick explained it's not just about third-party cookies, first-party cookies are at issue, too. 'The survey asked if users would be willing to share personal information with a trusted site in exchange for a more personalised experience,' Feick said. 'In the last year, there has been so much coverage about the potential compromise to personal data; we believe the results largely reflect that the survey took place amid coverage of these security breaches.'

The online survey was conducted in May 2005. It includes 923 respondents initially contacted via e-mail by online survey provider Zoomerang.

Understanding this context is important if you are to provide the desired service or product at the right time in the right place. Wrong customer data may lead to undesired 'personalised' services and unsatisfied customers. Several other problems are inherent to gathering and storing data from customers, such as privacy-sensitive information, determination of the relevance of gathered information, and legal and technological issues surrounding the exchange of this information. The Chameleon organisation is required to find adequate solutions for these problems.

The world of the 'clicks' enables the generation of customer information in this scenario, see Figure 4.2. Using it, a customer can increasingly be approached in a more targeted fashion, which can lead to stronger customer lock-in. Furthermore, it becomes possible to offer complementary products or services, for which the customer's interest can be inferred from their profile and/or the purchasing pattern.

REVENUE MODEL

The Chameleon essentially generates its revenues from transactions. These may include physical products that are delivered through traditional distribution channels, such as CD orders on the Internet, in which the ordering and payment take place on the Internet, with delivery via parcel service. Other products can be provided directly through the Internet since they are digital (software, movies or music). Organisations which are providing services and not products, can also adopt this business model. Banks and insurance companies for instance can efficiently offer mortgages, insurance and advice on these matters to their customers.

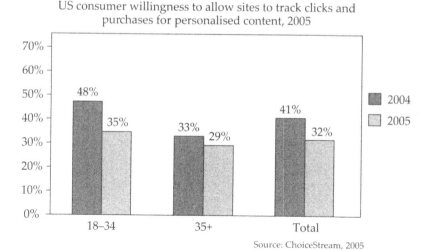

Figure 4.2   Tracking clicks and purchases

Another source of revenue may involve selling customer information. For a Chameleon organisation, this is counter-intuitive since selling customer information and profiles would directly affect their own competitive position. If organisations nevertheless opt to sell customer information and/or customer profiles as a source of revenue, they are choosing a different value model, see Figure 4.3. In practice, discussions on this subject will arise at a strategic level, when the organisation becomes aware of the fact that the customer information it offers is a valuable source of potential income. If companies decide to provide the customer information to third parties, it is of paramount importance that they protect the relationship with their customers. Customers do not generally provide their personal information with the goal of having it sold to third parties. Aspects of privacy and security are a growing concern and are beginning to play important roles in decisions of both customers and organisations.

DESIGN OF A CHAMELEON ORGANISATION

The design of a Chameleon organisation contains a number of contingency factors, design principles and processes. These are illustrated schematically in Figure 4.4.

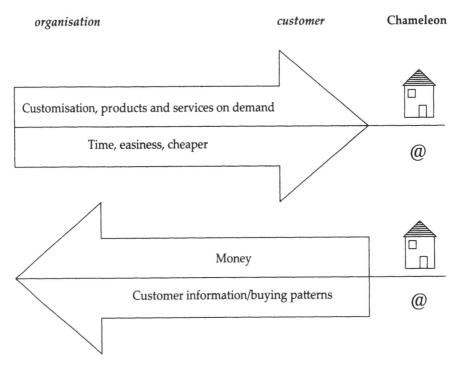

Figure 4.3   Value model for Chameleon

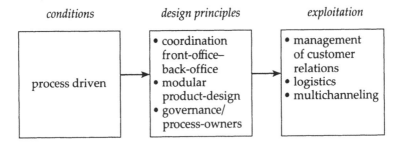

Figure 4.4   Design of the Chameleon

CONDITION

The most important contingency factor for the Chameleon business model is the capacity to think in terms of business processes. The need to redesign processes at the fundamental level is an essential difference between the Chameleon and more traditional business models, because the provision of customised products and services is tightly interwoven with the design of business processes.

DESIGN PRINCIPLES

The design principles of the Chameleon organisation primarily involve coordination between the following processes:

- the front-office and the back-office;

- the various modules of product or service;

- activities in the overall business process (governance in the form of process ownership).

COORDINATION BETWEEN FRONT-OFFICE AND BACK-OFFICE

De Vries (2003) points out that an organisation's front-office is the starting point for process-oriented organisation. It is here that the value the organisation has so carefully created in its business processes is transferred to the customer and where the organisation can display its customer focus. The front-office plays a crucial role in building relations with customers. It is also the point at which a service or product can be personalised (in a limited way) and where customer commitment can be realised in the form of personal relations. Although this process of personalisation can become rather complex, it can nevertheless be achieved, thanks to the availability of information on relationships, products and processes.

It is important to recognise that differences in the degree of customisation exist. Organisations face the choice of how far they are willing to go when it comes to offering customisation to customers. The choice for greater customisation not only affects the relation to the customer, but has direct consequences for the organisational design and the content and management of information as well. The model in Figure 4.5 distinguishes between five degrees of customisation and five matching types of front-offices. Since in the Chameleon business model mass customisation is the strategic choice, in principle the front-office type 'field and inside service' belongs to this business model. This strategy is designed to build relations and to fulfil transactions as cheaply as possible. The organisation delivers to the 'customised standardisation' customer, matched to the customer's needs. Product information is available on the level of standard components, along with information in the form of customer profiles. This affords the Chameleon organisation a pro-active approach to the customer.

By moving towards a greater degree of customisation (downwards in Figure 4.5) and therefore towards a more 'intimate' relationship with the customer, a transition to a different business model takes place. Thus, the Symbiosis' type of front-office tends towards an Innovator business model. As we will show in Chapter 6, the Foyer organisation does not fit within this scheme, because in that model the whole network is an integrated front-office and back-office at the same time.

Front-office type	Degree of customisation	Relation information	Product information
'counter'	Pure standardisation	Anonymous transactions	End products
'one-stop shop'	Segmented standardisation	Characteristics of market	Assortment
'field and inside service'	Customised standardisation	Customer profiles	Standard components
'control room'	Tailored customisation	Development of the relationship	Smallest replicable units
'symbiosis'	Pure customisation	Opportunities for partnership	Design knowledge

Figure 4.5   Front-office types

In redesigning processes you need to consider the links to external parties that play a role in these processes. If necessary, these need to be reshaped into more effective forms of collaboration. In the context of organisational efficiency, a choice of the Chameleon business model implies tight collaboration with other organisations. Generally this cooperation takes place in the back-office, which is the part of the organisation that does not come into direct contact with the customer, but is nonetheless responsible for (often a large) part of the total production process. There are, for example, organisations which manage websites and handle marketing, but fall back on a logistic service provider for the distribution and transport. Others collaborate with third party organisations to handle the billing via the Internet. These cases often involve long-term relations, in which the whole process is shaped by means of service level agreements and contracts. A large number of Internet stores follow this form of organisation. Parcel services and couriers have benefited tremendously from the advent of the Internet and the related sales of products through this channel.

MODULAR PRODUCTION

Mass customisation requires a dynamic network of relatively autonomous operational units. Each unit is responsible for a specific process or task, such as the production of a particular component or the execution of a particular stage

---

Personalised Shoes

Perhaps you have always dreamed about trendy but well-made shoes, perfectly formed to fit your own feet. Gretec is an organisation which delivers personalised shoes. The first time a customer enters the purchasing process, a model of their foot is made. Subsequently the customer determines the model of the shoe, the colour and the type of leather. The bespoke shoes will then be produced, based on the form of the customers feet and their personal wishes. The organisation stores the customer information during the transaction, to facilitate the next purchase.

---

of production. The parts of a product or service may be produced or supplied by third parties. The combination of the time and the manner of interaction in the production of a product or service may be different each time, depending on the needs and wishes of the customer. Without a modular product or service design, customisation of products in response to the wishes and demands of customers is very time-consuming and costly.

GOVERNANCE

In the Chameleon business model the governance is in the hands of the organisation. The customer has certain choices, but these choices are not fundamental, either for the strategy of the organisation, or for the design. The organisation decides which products/services are offered and defines the level of choice available. From time to time the choice of components is reviewed, and changes and modifications are made to the products/services. All initiatives for this process, however, lie with the organisation.

Another important aspect of governance in this business model is the management of the overall business process. The success of mass customisation is to a large extent dependent on the managerial qualities. In this dynamic, environment managers are responsible for the coordination of the various process steps, and for the coordination of the parties in the dynamic network. In the Chameleon organisation, process ownership is therefore a design variable. Managers have become process owners, meaning they no longer manage a department or business function, but rather a whole business process. Externally, both the customer and the collaborative partners are involved in this process. Internally, the governance model involves all the employees to add value to the process. Figure 4.6 depicts a possible design for a process oriented organisation. In this example we have chosen one back-office per process. However, in many

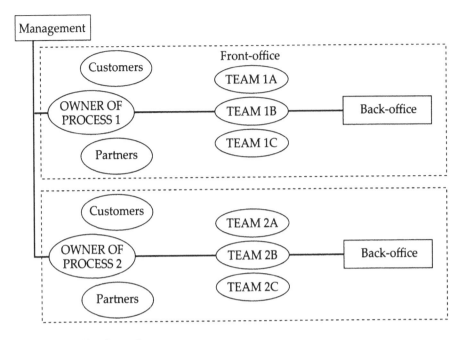

Figure 4.6   Design of a process

organisations, one back-office handling several business processes is more efficient, whether this is outsourced or not.

PROCESSES

The strategic choice for the Chameleon leads to an emphasis on the design of three processes, namely:

- the management of customer relations;
- the logistics;
- the coordination of the various distribution channels.

MANAGEMENT OF CUSTOMER RELATIONS

In a business model such as the Chameleon, in which the customer receives a personalised product or service, the management of customer relations takes a central place. As far as possible, the customer should be approached directly, even though this is not always possible due to the size of the market and the large number of transactions. The direct approach to the customer may be analysed and improved by means of the AIDA phase model.[1] A second helpful

---

1   AIDA is a helpful tool for market communication, more specifically for direct marketing. The initial characters reflect the essence of the model:

starting point for a Chameleon organisation is the Market Space Model (Dutta and Segev 1999) we described in Chapter 2. The four Ps discussed there can replace the four steps of AIDA.

The first step of AIDA involves gaining attention. With the rise of the Internet, the quantity of information any potential customer has access to has increased significantly. Your ability to gain a customer's attention for your own organisation is therefore essential. However, mere attention is not sufficient. For the Chameleon organisation, attracting attention relies on customer information, because it allows a more personal approach to the customer. For example, current customers can be notified of new product developments via e-mail, or current readers can be forewarned if a new book by their favourite author is being published. In the Four Ps model, this step, the P 'influence on promotion' is relevant: online promotion; customer-focused promotion campaigns and online advertisement.

Attention needs to generate interest (step 2). The real issue in this step is not so much the description of the product or new product properties, but rather a clarification of why the new offer will be advantageous for the consumer. The organisation might join an (independent) virtual community of users to emphasise such a message, or to generate ideas for improvements from the customers themselves. A virtual community of customers may even be initiated and/or facilitated by the organisation, in which case the organisation is moving towards the Foyer business model.

The third step is the creation of a need or desire. The offer needs to be irresistible to the customer. Free products, samples or demonstration copy are all strategies for whetting the customers' appetite. Offering an extra service is another, such as access to invoices on the Internet. Providing tips on useful by-products or on how to use products or services can also encourage the demand. This relates to the P of the Market Space model: 'influence on the product'. Examples include: online product catalogue, extra information on products, online aid in the search for a product and product customisation.

Pharmaceutical companies like Merck offer customers online services in the form of product guides that inform customers about the use of the products. Merck also provides detailed information on a multitude of physical

A = Attention
I = Interest
D = Desire
A = Action

complaints, symptoms, remedies and the relevant Merck medicines. Interactive quizzes keep the customers interested. Also, professionals in health care are able to exchange information via online forums (Dutta and Segev 1999).

The fourth step is the transition to action. Once the customer's attention has been gained, the customer has become convinced of the advantages and a desire to act has been created, it is time to guide the customer into the actual transaction. At this stage it is important to make sure that buying the product is simple. This relates to the P 'influence on place' in the Market Space model: online ordering of products, real-time processing of orders, online payment and online product distribution. Multiple methods of payment are offered as well. This refers to the P 'influence on price': price information is available online and special price arrangements can be made for each individual customer. The Chameleon organisation will use customer profiles for this, greatly facilitating the ordering and billing. The customer, after all, is already known and the Chameleon already has the customer information.

The role of the Internet and IT in the management of the whole interaction process has been described in the business model of Dutta and Segev (1999) as: influence on Customer Relationship Management (CRM) by means of feedback of the customer and the online customer service. A good example of the management of customer relations was described in the case at the beginning of the chapter about Hilton Hotels.

THE LOGISTICS PROCESS

Mass customisation is not possible without an efficiently designed logistics and IT process. Logistics contribute directly to the basic idea behind the Chameleon model: efficiency and personalisation. The complexity that is inherent in mass customisation requires coordination of the entire process. The design of logistical processes needs to facilitate and simplify this process.

Logistics deserve further attention because most organisations are faced with the challenge of handling multi-channelling (provision of products or services to customers by various distribution channels). The question of how to coordinate various channels is discussed separately later in this section.

LOGISTICS AND COMPLEXITY

Because of customised production and the increasing unpredictability of the market, production is becoming more difficult to manage since the processes of forecasting and central planning are now unreliable. For this reason, the static concept of a chain fits more appropriately to traditional business models.

Personalisation places large demands on logistic support, because managing the combination of various components from various parties is highly complex. Process flexibility needs to be supported by logistic and IT-processes. Logistics nearly always involve both a physical and an information flow. A consequence of the fact that products/services are adapted for the requirements of different customers is that they need to be identifiable during the entire process. Standardisation of this process and the use of the Internet for the storage of the basic data (the information flow) form the starting point if you are to ensure an efficient system.

To guarantee flexibility and to prevent the problem of being physically distant from the customer, the Chameleon organisation often uses external warehouses and distribution centres for the tasks of packaging and distribution. Fixed costs can be reduced in this manner in times of uncertain demand. In order to outsource part of the logistical process, it is necessary to establish integration between the information systems of all partners. This is particularly complex when the situation involves a large number of parties, such as suppliers of parts, companies that assemble parts and those responsible for final assembly. The Internet can make a contribution to the efficiency of logistical processes. By streamlining the ordering process through the Internet the transaction costs will be much lower, and will even amount up to only half of the costs inherent to sales by means of a catalogue (Gulati and Garino 2000).

COORDINATION OF DISTRIBUTION CHANNELS

Strategic decisions about customer relations must also address the question of which channels can be used to promote customisation. Information technology has opened up new possibilities for distribution of products and services via more and/or new channels. This is referred to as 'multi channelling' (De Vries 2003). The Chameleon organisation needs to ensure a proper coordination between the various channels, so that the right customer can be reached and serviced in the most effective manner, see Figure 4.7.

Small start-ups may choose the Chameleon business model and expand to become larger organisations whose core activity lies in the sales of products and services on the Internet. On the other hand, we also see a lot of existing organisations opting for a Chameleon business model. In an attempt to acquire market share in the same area of business that it has been a player for years in 'the real physical world'. The Chameleon organisation is often focused on

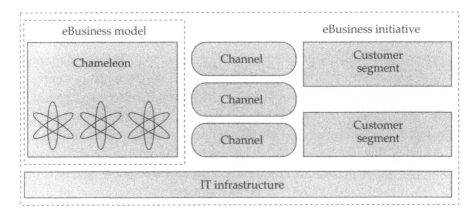

Figure 4.7   Channel coordination

the sale of tangible products/services that have been marketed for years via other distribution channels. However, as soon as these organisations adopt the Chameleon model, the customer usually enjoys greater choice of components or parts that are to be included in the complete product or service. Examples of this can be found in nearly all Internet shopping sites and bookings for services, such as in the Hilton case, fall within this business model as well. Purchases or bookings through the Internet need some added value over the traditional purchases, such as convenience for the customer or lower costs. The problem for the Chameleon that presents itself is finding solutions for potential coordination problems concerning the utilisation of multiple distribution channels. If you are used to working with agents, as is common in financial services, problems can arise when you are selling directly, because this will harm the business of your own agents.

The question of the choice of distribution channels is complex. It involves not only the process phases, market segments to be serviced and media that should be used but the prices, target groups, and so on all need to be considered as well. Ultimately, this means that the business will need to focus on the coordination of channels along which it wishes to service its customers. De Vries (2003) points out that flexible coordination of different channels needs to be possible, in order to open up the appropriate product range (in terms of the assortment and degree of customisation) with the appropriate performance, via focused communication, to the appropriate market segments.

The problem of multi-channelling becomes more complex, as:

- multiple phases in the production or service delivery process are distinguished;

- the depth of segmentation of the market increases;

- the supply of channels through which customers may access the product or service increases;

- the product range becomes broader and more tailored to individual customer demands;

- the communication with the customer is more focused on the personal relationship;

- higher demands are made of the capacity of channel co-ordination.

The selection of a particular distribution channel remains a complicated issue, since so many factors must be taken into consideration simultaneously. The choice in channel configuration (IT and architecture) one makes must therefore be carefully weighed up.

INFORMATION AND COMMUNICATION TECHNOLOGY

Information and communication technology (IT) should support both an organisation's strategic choices and the processes that are designed to achieve the chosen strategy. In the following section we will elaborate on the role of IT support needed for the Chameleon organisation. In the first part, we offer a number of questions, the answers to which may facilitate the selection of the appropriate IT-applications. In the second part we will discuss a number of applications that are often associated with a Chameleon business model (see Figure 4.8).

FOCUS OF IT-APPLICATIONS

The focus of the IT-applications of the Chameleon organisation must be on both an efficient execution of the internal processes and on the relationship with the environment (customers, suppliers and partners).

INTERNAL FOCUS

An organisation that opts for the Chameleon business model may find it useful to consider the following questions around the efficient streamlining of processes:

- What is the total runtime for the delivery of the product or service?

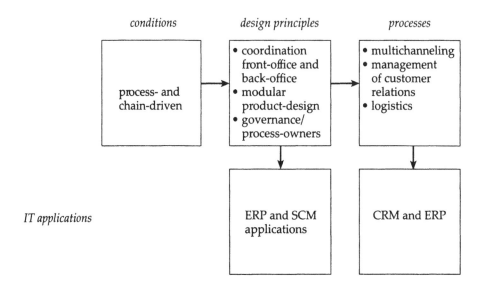

Figure 4.8   Design and IT of Chameleon

- What are the waiting periods in between the various process phases?

- How much slack is present in the total process?

- Is there redundancy of data?

- What causes production or service errors?

- How many complaints are reported and what do they cover?

Improvements in the process can be initiated based on these questions, or rather on the answers to them. Questions that can guide these changes include:

- How can IT help in the reduction of the waiting periods?

- How can slack be reduced by implementation of IT?

- Is it possible to reduce runtimes?

- How can the number of complaints be reduced?

EXTERNAL FOCUS

Information about how customers behave is the most relevant reciprocal value of the Chameleon model. Questions to ask in order to explore this behaviour can include:

- Who buys these products/services and in what form(s)?

- What customer segments can be distinguished?

- When (time, season) do which target groups buy?

- How often do customers visit a website before they engage in a transaction?

- Which methods of payment do they use?

- Which distribution channel do customers choose and/or prefer for delivery?

- How did customers arrive at the company website?

- Which offers do customers respond to?

This information can lead to the kind of forward looking questions, in which IT might fulfil a supportive role:

- Which product components for customisation can be offered?

- What payment options should be offered?

- Which products/services can be offered to specific target groups?

- How can you approach your customers?

- Which delivery options should be offered?

The following questions may be useful for exploring relationships with suppliers or partners:

- What elements of the product or service can be delivered by a supplier or are 'produced' by a partner?

- What are the delivery requirements (speed, location, etc.)?

- How does supplier communication take place?

- Is direct data exchange with your partner possible?

IT-APPLICATIONS

Internal Focus: Enterprise Resource Planning (ERP)

The Chameleon organisation relies on an efficient production and delivery of products and services. This, in turn, requires an optimal support of processes by IT. Enterprise Resource Planning (ERP) focuses on the integration of data, related to the various company functions in an organisation. The high level of integration that can be accomplished by the implementation of ERP-systems implies a trade-off with flexibility. However, developers of ERP-systems increasingly take into account the flexibility needed to enable changes. These changes are mainly focused on the development of connections to external oriented systems, such as customer relationship management (CRM) systems. Thus it becomes possible to combine the internal focus of ERP- and SCM-systems (discussed in the next section) with the external focus of CRM systems (Malhotra 2000).

Internal Focus: Supply Chain Management (SCM)

Striving for efficiency is not confined to one organisation, but concerns the entire production or service delivery chain. Coordination will need to take place between all participants. SCM has a primarily internal focus, although increasingly more attention is devoted to the relationships with suppliers and partners. SCM concerns the coordination of the 'chain of economic actions that together form the components of the final manufactured product' (Peppers et al. 1999). SCM is a logistical concept that often serves as the foundation for information systems that spawn under the name of SCM as well. SCM concerns chain management, enabling an increase of efficiency. The goal is to reduce (coordination) problems among the various steps of a process and manage the entire chain as well. Despite the fact that SCM is based on the more static chain-concept, the term also goes well with the logistical network idea of the Chameleon model. Every order by a customer can be regarded by itself as a temporary chain that needs to be managed.

External Focus: Customer Relationship Management (CRM)

Producing at as low a cost as possible is a condition for delivering low prices. Customers are demanding choices from the characteristics of a product or service, which require insight into the customer's profile, as already pointed out in this chapter. Support of this process by IT-applications, for instance in the form of CRM, can contribute. 'Customer Relationship Management describes the activities an organisation engages in, in order to identify, qualify, attract and develop relations with loyal and profitable customers, by delivering the right product or right service at the right time, through the right channel' (Galbreath 1999).

Information systems have been developed around CRM and they are often referred to by the same name. CRM-systems construct a database of customers and their buying behaviour. Using advanced techniques, not openly obvious buying patterns can be discerned from the database. This process is referred to by the term 'data mining'. Subsequently, an organisation can act pro-actively on these patterns to make customer offers that are tailored to buying behaviour.

CONCLUSIONS

The Chameleon business model, of all three types in this book, has most in common with traditional business models. The important difference, however, is the way in which opportunities of information technology and the changing demands of the customers, lead Chameleon organisations to offer customised products and services. Managers and employees are familiar with the underlying design principles, precisely because of the connection to more traditional ways of doing business. The model visibly generates short-term profits, when compared to the other two business models. In Chapter 7 this issue is discussed more in depth.

CHAPTER 5

The Innovator Model

The environment in which organisations operate is currently going through changes at breakneck pace. In many cases the changes involve fundamental breaks with previous developments. To be successful in the growing global economy of the 21st century, organisations are obliged to develop new products and services continuously. In this age of permanent innovation, knowledge is the crucial asset. An explosive growth of knowledge and cheap transfer of that knowledge through the Internet and other media, combine to form a fertile soil for virtually unlimited innovation. The fact that organisations are confronted with all kinds of unpredictable changes has become a rule rather than an exception. This means that many organisations need to focus not only on innovation, as a direct condition for survival in the today's world, but also on choosing an innovative business model. This is the 'the Innovator' business model.

The Innovator: Case Study Access Point

Access Point is an interactive information system that is voice- and touch-controlled. It allows people to both obtain information and communicate via the Internet, and to execute transactions via a multi-media terminal. Access Point uses the most elementary communication tool, the human voice, as an interface with the extended world of information on the net. Speech recognition is complemented by a 'touch screen'. Supported by the Access Point system, in Vienna (where a pilot is running) people currently have access to information ranging from questions about new apartments, to how one can apply for passports, or where the nearest child care centre is. Access Point signifies a breakthrough in technology, meaning that it brings to the market a totally new and different solution. The revolution in technology is, in this case, the AP-communicator, a voice-operated Internet browser, that forms the core of the entire system.

Access Point arose from a joint venture of Philips Multi Media and LB-data, an Austrian PC-company. Being a small and flexible company, it is embedded in the extensive Philips Matrix, allowing it to profit from the extensive international network and the superior portfolio of technologies. The fact that Access Point is free from the tight control of the Philips organisation affords it the leeway to build network relations. Access Point's rapidly developing and self-organising network environment needs to be able to develop at the same pace as the technological innovation. Minimal rules must therefore be imposed on the internal governance and the management of relation-developing processes of Access Point. The system unites a large number of parties whose interests are shared. The resources of Access Point are largely knowledge-based and mainly lie outside of the borders of the 'parental' company and Philips itself. This is characteristic of situations in which breakthrough technologies create an opportunity for new innovative applications. Moreover, the environment demands a certain extent of leeway in the capacities and tools to guarantee a greater degree of adaptation to the inevitable changes that are taking place. Other network participants that are stakeholders in the particular market space must be identified. Access Point needs to estimate to what extent the various interests can be coordinated, establish a workable consensus, and coordinate activities to promote the mutual well-being of the participants. The capacity to adapt to the network needs to developed by and spread through the network. Superior technology is, after all, rarely sufficient for the establishment of a strong enough competitive position. But the most important task lying before Access Point is to succeed in capturing the imagination of the interest groups in the network – including the customers – so that these groups wish to take part in the creation of an extraordinary vision for the future of the network community.

(Tovstiga and Fantner 2000)

INTRODUCTION

In this chapter we discuss the Innovator, the second business model in our typology. Innovation is clearly not a new phenomenon. Yet a number of new developments can be identified that place the spotlight on innovations more than ever before.

The first reason for the need for innovation is a shift in the current economy from profits from scarcity to the *entrepreneurial* profits as a basis for profitability. Entrepreneurial profits are those made by innovating organisations in the period between the introduction of a new product onto the market, and the moment that it becomes available on the market on a large scale. Entrepreneurial profits are temporary, and can be generated by many sources.

A second, related reason, is the phenomenon that organisations with traditional business models are trying to provide ever more products and services at ever lower prices. This strategy continuously pushes up the costs of labour and scarce resources. At the same time, customers expect to pay less, due to the abundance of what is on offer. As a consequence, products and services are becoming commoditised; only the price is distinctive to the customer. Many organisations finds themselves caught in a downward spiral. Continuous innovation, providing customers with ever more added value, seems to be the answer (Abraham and Knight 2001).

The Innovator business model is devoted to realising innovations. The design of an Innovator organisation involves a group of people and parties who share information, ideas, experiences and insights, with the expectation that all parties will gain from their cooperation.

The following section is devoted to the concept of 'innovation', which forms the core of this business model. We then focus on the strategy behind the Innovator. One of the decisive conditions for an effective innovation process is the involvement of the right customers in the right way. This condition is discussed in the market communication section. Although every Innovator will be of a unique design, we present a number of design principles that are generally applicable. We also explore the role IT plays in the model along with the important question of how an organisation or individual can enter or adapt to this business model.

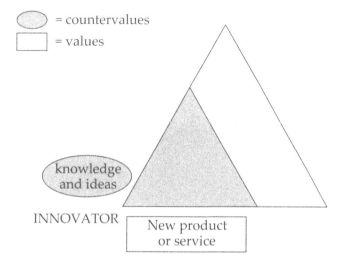

Figure 5.1   Business model Innovator

INNOVATION

Innovation is a complicated and varied phenomenon. It may involve products or services, processes, markets, management and organisation practices. It can be based on aesthetic or social ideals. Innovation knows many facets; various types of knowledge and skills, and all kinds of visions can contribute to innovation (Kalthoff et al. 1997). There is therefore no *one* way to achieve and 'organise' innovation. An organisation and/or network can be innovative in the very choice of an innovation-process. Nonetheless, there are discernible patterns that may serve as a helpful tool for participants of an Innovator organisation and enable them to establish a firm process.

DEFINITIONS OF INNOVATION

Despite some differences, the authors who focus on the concept of innovation agree on a number of points. For instance, they deem knowledge to be an extremely important aspect, but agree that knowledge in itself is not the same as innovation. The concept of knowledge has content at its core, whereas innovation evolves around the process (Amidon 1997). Innovation involves the uniting of various sources of knowledge and skills, which together provide a catalyst to the process. Innovation only takes place when a commercial application is discovered, as shown in Figure 5.2.

This is reinforced by the following definition: Innovation is a process involving multiple activities performed by multiple actors from one or several organisations featuring new combinations of means and/or ends to old and/or new market-partners (Hauschildt 1997).

Another aspect of innovation that receives a lot of attention is its type. Generally, two fundamentally different types of innovation are distinguished: *structural* and *incremental* innovation. 'Structural' innovation entails the creation

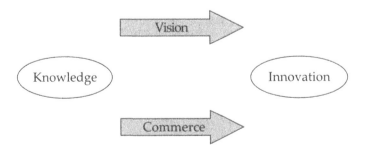

Figure 5.2   From Knowledge to Innovation

of genuinely new products or services (and the process by which they are created), that are radically different from existing products or services. This innovation is also referred to by the terms 'disruptive innovation' or 'breakthrough innovation'. It contrasts with a gradual adaptation and improvement of existing products or services, which is referred to as 'incremental innovation'. Other authors advocate more nuances, distinguish between multiple innovation levels and include structural and incremental innovation as the extremes on the scale.[1]

Nintendo's Innovation Challenge

President Satoru Iwata took the stage in front of 3,000 developers and press members and delivered a speech that detailed just how important innovation, change and disruption can be for the industry. Rather than go head to head with its rivals in current market sectors, the firm plans on reinventing the way players currently relate to games. Since the launch of the Nintendo DS, the company has successfully managed to 'disrupt' the game industry by releasing a product that is very different from any other console currently available. He talked specifically about success of the Brain Training series of games which has captured a brand new demographic of gamers in Japan. By believing that people wanted something new and different to play and by actually making non-gamers sit down and play the game, it became apparent that disrupting the typical methods of game development and publishing paid off and tapped into a whole new market of consumers. Iwata's enduring theme was to challenge game designers to create new methods of game creation, leading to innovation and broader demographic appeal.

(Game Developers Conference 2006)

The Innovator organisation is essentially positioned towards the middle ground on such a scale. A network of involved parties develops applications for

---

1 For instance, Clark and Staunton (1989) present the following five levels:
   - Generic innovations that create new techno-paradigms, out of which clusters of innovations arise from a new core process (electricity, steam engines, the microchip) that cut across sectors and stages of production.
   - 'Epochal' innovations (innovations belonging to a period), that remain confined as part of the generic innovation to specific sectors, for example the development of the automatic transmission in the car industry.
   - Dynamic innovations, that introduce important changes on the organisational level, such as the electronic register system.
   - Continuing innovations that change existing methods, but proceed in the same direction.
   - Incremental innovations, where there are no new inputs, but where the existing collection of inputs is reformed in order to enhance the performance of the system.

a new technology. Incidentally, the activities an Innovator organisation engages in need not always involve breakthrough technologies or practices. These imply innovations that signify drastically new developments and improvements for the customer and/or other participants in the Innovator model.

INNOVATION PROCESS

Aside from the taxonomy of types of innovation, a distinction is made in the innovation process. It is interesting to consider whether or not there is a difference between the idea/invention, the commercial application and the distribution of innovations, in the business model Innovator. The ideal type of Innovator organisation discussed in this chapter focuses only on the first two phases. As soon as an innovation is implemented, it is 'exploited' in another business model, such as the Chameleon model. In practice, the Innovator then ceases to exist or redirects its attention – often in different composition – to new innovations.

STRATEGY

> To understand and evolve innovation, it must be studied as a process
> – a series of steps that produce a desired result. To that end, innovation
> can be defined as a process for creating new and significant customer
> value (Ulwick and Eisenhauer I 2000)

If an organisation chooses innovation, there are certain consequences for the value model; for the way revenues are generated by the innovations, and for the way the market is involved in the creation of innovations. A characteristic of the Innovator organisation is that the innovation is supported by the entire network of co-creating organisations and customers.

VALUES

Two types of customers can be distinguished in the Innovator model. The first type is customers who will buy and use the products or services the Innovator organisation produces at an early stage. These customers are referred to as 'Early Adopters'. Innovation is driven by these early adopters. In some cases they may even be the ones to provide initial financing. The second type of customer is a participant in the network: a customer who has chosen cooperation with others, either because of an overwhelming customer need for innovation products or service, or because the participant is motivated to realise an idea that they were responsible for developing. In the latter case, the interests of the customer, as 'co-creator' are largely identical to the interests of the other participants in the network, namely the realisation of the innovation and a fair allocation of the generated revenues. The values and reciprocal values of both types, the customers and the other participants, differ. This is why they are discussed in two separate sections.

VALUE MODEL CUSTOMERS

The most important value the Innovator model offers the customers as end-users, is the fact that thanks to innovation, they receive radically new products or services. Offering something *new* is the goal and basis of the Innovator organisation. In the Western world, where products or services of high quality are widely available, customers product choice is guided by other features, such as novelty or advanced technology. There is a substantial group of wealthy customers for whom access to new products and services is of great value. This use of innovation provides the customer with a feeling of sophistication. This is not a tangible benefit, yet increasingly important in a world in which emotion and experience dictate choices. The experience can be enhanced via the Internet through virtual communities, where customers are able to share their experiences of the innovations.

The *reciprocal value* that is delivered to the Innovator organisation are the revenues, either direct or indirect, that come through exploitation of

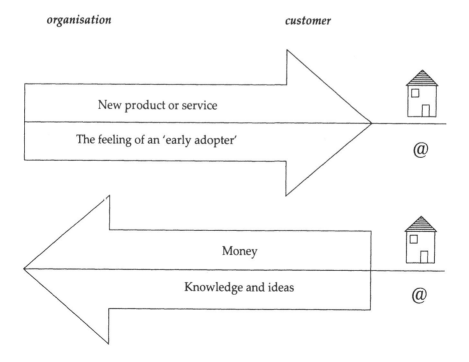

Figure 5.3   Value model for the Innovator and customers

the innovation. A second, very important, reciprocal value are the insights, experiences and ideas of the customers themselves. Promotional activities are important as well. These can be generated through the Internet, either in virtual communities or otherwise. This means that the exploiter needs to be involved with the Innovator as much as possible, preferably as a fully-fledged participant. The exploiter of the innovation (the organisation that brings the innovation to the market), after all, has the most direct relation to the customers of the innovative product or the innovative service, and is also the one that manages the knowledge and ideas of the customers. Incidentally, these do not entail ideas about incremental improvements, but offer real, structurally innovative insights and suggestions from customers. Should the exploiter prove to be unwilling or unable to provide this, then the Innovator itself might create a virtual community to mobilise users of the innovations. This would also serve as a (partial) solution for the problem that this business model faces with the, very temporary, lock-in of the consumers of its products. After all, the newness of these kinds of innovations disappears as soon as other organisations market the same products or services.

VALUE MODEL PARTICIPANTS

The principle *value* the Innovator model offers its participants is synergy of knowledge and ideas. Innovations are only possible these days by uniting different sources of knowledge and skills. An Innovator organisation is a

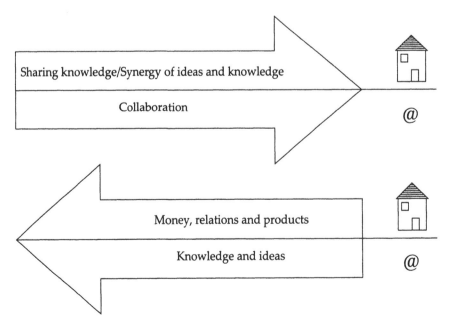

Figure 5.4   Value model for the Innovator and participants

collection of complementary core competencies, which realise an innovation in mutual collaboration. In this sense, the Innovator model more accurately resembles the Japanese way of innovation, rather than that practised by more familiar Western organisations.

> Western creativity is based on the idea of individual freedom and expression. It appears analogous to nuclear fission where individual atoms produce energy; contrarily, Japanese energy resembles nuclear fusion, where particles must join together to create a reaction (Amidon 1997).

Another reason for the collaboration of parties is the aspiration to unite the Innovator partners from different networks.

Narry Singh, Vice-president of Global Trading:

> It's no longer about the core competencies of partners or what their companies do. It's more about their affiliation and who they know. Who do they collaborate with, and who can they influence? That makes a real difference, especially in terms of entering new markets (Levy 2001).

There is another important *reciprocal value* offered by the participants to the Innovator, aside from knowledge itself, and this is the connections and networks in which they participate independently. The Innovator functions in a network environment, where competitive advantage often depends on skilled management of the various mutual beneficial relations in the network.

REVENUE MODEL

The revenues for the Innovator model are generated either through sales of (patents of) innovations, or by the subsequent exploitation of these innovations in the form of another business model. In the latter, one or several of the participants in the model may take responsibility for production and/or delivery of the product or service. Since the Innovator organisation is a network, an important and potentially problematic issue is the allocation of revenues. The Innovator needs to strike a balance between, on the one hand, formulating clear agreements, and on the other, ensuring sufficient flexibility to accommodate changes in these agreements. After all, the innovative process is first and foremost unpredictable.

MARKET COMMUNICATION

> Ironically, it's the firms with the strongest customer relationships that find it the hardest to convert disruptive technologies into new revenue

> *streams. It's not that pleasing your best customers is itself dangerous,*
> *but pleasing them exclusively means that the growth opportunities*
> *presented by new markets will go ignored and uncultivated (Christensen*
> *1997).*

Deciding which customers ought to be involved in the innovation process, and how, is one of the key factors in the process. For the involvement of customers in the innovations and/or the innovative applications, it is imperative that the parties in the Innovator approach the right market(s) with the appropriate questions.

In an ideal situation, organisations provide most value(s) to customers who they themselves value most. Determination of which value(s) a customer wishes to receive turns out to be a substantial problem in the realisation of innovation, despite the fact that organisations invest vast amounts of time, effort and financial resources into the matter. One of the obstacles lies in the way organisations divide their market into market segments. Segmentation is generally based on demographics, size, or vertical branches, such as traditional industry categorisations (transport, telecommunication, energy and so on). Organisations need to discover for each customer group which value(s) they wish to receive. The traditional categorisation entails that customers who want completely different values are grouped together and that customers who wish to receive similar values are divided into different segments. This supplies the organisation or the network with contradictory or incoherent information. Asking the wrong customers thereby prevents the network from gathering the information and knowledge from the segments that is essential for innovation (Ulwick and Eisenhauer I 2000). For organisations this implies a fundamentally different perspective on market communication. To identify the coherence among customers, (network-) organisations may, for instance, employ communities that are set up by the organisation/network or by the customers themselves. Here, incidentally, the Innovator is making steps in the direction of the business model Foyer, which is discussed in Chapter 6.

ASKING THE WRONG QUESTIONS

A second problem is the way communication with customers takes place. In most cases, customers are asked for their opinions on products or services that are provided and any requests for improvements, and so on. However, this is not usually an area where they have much experience. The common complaint: 'Customers don't know what they want' is usually as a result of asking the wrong questions. Customers are experts on the processes for which they employ the solutions (products or services), or for which they desire better solutions. For example, customers are interested in and knowledgeable about the food they give to their family or helping their children to learn. If you ask them for opinions on or improvements to cooking stoves, lawn mowers and textbooks, the chances are that they will never have little of value to feedback. Organisations think in terms of solutions that can be developed on the basis of own expertise and core competencies, and that can be improved incrementally (Ulwick and Eisenhauer II 2000).

The focus on 'own solutions from own expertise' is therefore often the biggest obstacle for more drastic innovation. It also explains in part why innovative solutions to the real need(s) of the customers, namely *innovative improvement to the customer processes*, are almost exclusively developed by the customers and/or in cooperation with the customers and partner organisations in a network.

Inventions by Customers (von Hippel 2000)

- Mountain bike
- Protein shampoo
- Sports bra
- Chocolate milk
- E-mail
- Desktop Publishing

INVOLVING THE WRONG GROUPS OF PARTNERS

Organisations need to focus on their core competencies. What they and their customers don't know can be learned through intensive collaboration in the network. This process involves marrying customer competencies with the competencies of other participants in the network. In this context Christensen's (1997) warning (as described at the beginning of this section), should be kept in mind. The customers who need to be involved in the process of innovation are not always in the organisation's category of 'regular customers'. For example:

> A team, focused on structural innovation for bandages (used postoperatively), agreed that the process for which a solution needed to be found was the control of infections. Due to the involvement of experts and customers in these innovations, the team discovered that specialists in veterinary hospitals were able to control the level of infection in spite of difficult circumstances and limited financial resources. As one of the most prominent veterinarians explained to the team: 'Our patients are

covered with hair, don't bathe and have no medical insurance, which means that measures for infection control cannot be too costly.' (Von Hippel 2000)

A caveat is that the more participants are involved, the more costly the network will become in terms of time, knowledge sharing and direct financial investment. Innovation remains an in-depth investment.

DESIGN OF THE INNOVATOR ORGANISATION: NETWORKING IS THE KEY

The actual design of the Innovator organisation will be different in every situation. Over time this design will change as a result of reaction and adaptation to the dynamics. Nevertheless, there are a number of common developments in the design of an innovative business model that can be identified. Their global direction was outlined in 1997 by Amidon in her description of the fifth generation organisation, which she referred to as the design of the new millennium. The new organisations are a mix of conscious design on the one hand and natural

---

Fifth Generation Organisations

Systems need to work together rather than compete. The focus on the whole innovative system needs to include suppliers, distributors and other stakeholders including customers and competitors. Such Strategic Business Systems operate amongst kaleidoscopic changes, the temporal dynamics of which will increase. The success of organisations will be measured in terms of intellectual assets and the capacity to generate and apply new ideas in a rapidly changing market. Symbiotic learning networks – electronic and human – are as essential to daily operation as they are to the formulation of the business strategy. All participants in the innovative system are self-motivating and responsible for the creation of new knowledge as a way of contributing value for the organisation and the customers. Managers will monitor the flow of knowledge with an energy comparable to the amount previously invested in the management of capital, parts and material flows. IT, with sophisticated computer and communication systems, will include knowledge processing capacities that support learning and spread knowledge towards all participants in the entire enterprise. Knowledge is the asset that needs to be managed, and a new focus on customer success is a progressive way of creating a future together.

(Amidon 1997)

and uncontrolled dynamic systems on the other hand. She suggests that current practice is a combination of naturally developing 'ecological' systems of all kinds of stakeholders and carefully designed schematics in organisations for profitable growth. It is precisely this combination that creates value (Amidon 1997). The challenge for organisations and networks is to make the right choices in continuously changing circumstances.

Figure 5.5 displays the design principles that are the foundations for the network form of the Innovator organisation.

CONDITIONS

> *The design and practice of organisation can be accomplished to provide a base for constant innovation. These are created from the cognitive step of realising that innovation is a matter of organisation and then designing so that the requirements are met by the operation of the system itself rather than by special effort 'against' the system (McMaster 1998).*

The design principles behind an Innovator organisation are unusual. For instance, the realisation of trust, a social contract and a collective ambition, are conditions that need to be met to a sufficiently high degree before the innovation process can start and these principles will require continued attention once the organisation is up and running. The creation of virtual teams and communities and the establishment of a network of relations between participants underpin the design principles and define the ultimate

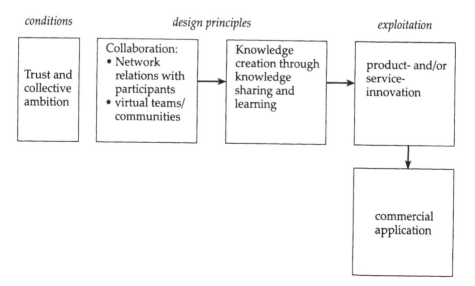

Figure 5.5   Design of the Innovator

shape that the organisation assumes. Finally, the innovation process involves the organisation of learning and knowledge sharing. This combination of design and process leads to innovation and subsequently to the commercial application of the innovations.

TRUST AND SOCIAL CONTRACT

Many organisations tend to fall back on control mechanisms in times or situations of uncertainty. For example, they use contracts in which clear agreements about expectations and duties are delineated. In the Innovator business model such an approach is counterproductive, as it hampers the nature of innovation. There are two reasons for this. The first is found in the nature of the process. Because of the unpredictability of innovation and the uncertainty of the results, fixed arrangements are (almost) impossible to secure. The second reason lies in the nature of the knowledge shared by participants in the model. This entails, inter alia, knowledge about systematic innovation that is codified and formalised. Examples can be found in technical descriptions of innovative technologies such as nanotechnology, biomedical technology and so on. However, most of the knowledge will be tacit knowledge that is hard for others to imitate (Nonaka and Takeuchi 1995). This tacit knowledge is the fundamental reason why the Innovator model depends on a network of participants. As this implicit knowledge can hardly, if at all, be expressed in a formal manner, no legal or procedural protective measures exist (de Laat 2000).

Innovation generally takes place in a complex and turbulent environment. This means that the outcome of a total innovative process is uncertain and unpredictable. This is the case both because of the mutual interdependence of participants, and also because of the need to share knowledge – one of the most valuable resources of an organisation – with partners.

Thus partners in the network are obliged to engage in a relationship of considerable trust. They need to work together because none of the partners is by themselves capable of achieving the goal of innovation. Trust can be defined as the mutual readiness of parties to be interdependent with a feeling of relative safety (McKnight et al. 1998). The role of trust in this form of organisation is so significant that authors have even started to consider trust as a coordination mechanism (Jarvenpaa and Shaw 1998). This means that you can use this in a deliberate way in your organisation design to ensure coordination of activities. Kogut and Zander (1996) point out that trust is essential to the transfer of knowledge. This makes the requirement of trust among participants one of the most characteristic elements of the Innovator model. Measures to build trust in the Innovator include:

- consistency over time (consistent operation increases reliability and predictability)

- integrity: coherence in words and deeds

- communication and openness

- genuine care and attention to each other

- shared governance.

Building this trust demands time and effort and rarely leads to immediately visible results. But this is nonetheless crucial to ensure an open attitude amongst all participants and their willingness to share knowledge. In this regard, one can speak of entering into a social contract, among or instead of other more formal contracts. In the social contract, each party shows willingness to make itself dependent on other participants and agrees to not abuse the dependent position of the other participant(s). It remains crucial for all parties to be aware of the most important role and purpose of the contract: to enable participants to volunteer and share knowledge. Ensuring this willingness to contribute knowledge requires the following design principle:

COLLECTIVE AMBITION

> *Formation of shared will is the most rare and least tangible of the three sources of networked community-building. It happens in conversations in which participants form and articulate a common intention. 'Communities of commitment' and 'communities of creation' revolve around what people care about and want to create together. However, most discussions about setting goals, targets and objectives do not qualify as the formation of shared will. Negotiations about targets and objectives do not create community. The formation of shared will does (Scharmer 2000).*

An important design principle that is closely related to the previous one is the requirement of collective ambition amongst all participants. The participants in the Innovator organisation need to aspire to a common goal, the realisation of an agreed innovation. This is referred to by different terms such as the 'shared dream', 'shared will', 'strategic intention' or 'collective ambition'. All authors agree on this: it is the collective ambition that binds the participants.

This all sounds very noble. Amidon (1997) nevertheless points to practice, where competition, conflicts of interest and differences of opinion are the rule rather than the exception. This complication increases in scope and severity if the situation involves cross-organisational cooperation, which is why a common innovative vision (shared dream) is crucial.

The foremost task for managers in the Innovator is the realisation of this collective ambition and the need to build trust among all participants in the network. Managers need to commit strongly to the realisation of a shared identity for the network in which their organisations function, and to the kind of communication that is vital to this process. This task requires good social skills of the managers involved.

STRUCTURE OF THE INNOVATOR

> *Japanese companies have long been working in alliances for the sole purpose of learning from each other, and without expecting direct economic returns. This concept is utterly alien to Western corporate life (Amidon 1997).*

NETWORK RELATIONS AMONG THE PARTICIPANTS

An important lock-in problem for the Innovator is the binding of the various parties in the Innovator. When are customers willing to co-design products or services that will benefit others? When are allied organisations and sometimes even competitors willing to share knowledge? The reason why participants prove amenable to cooperate within the context of innovation – without certainty of direct profit – has a number of causes. We have already mentioned various developments that gave rise to this phenomenon. There are a number of reasons why innovations take place in a network:

- The customer often demands innovative products or services that are common to various industries.

- The market often requires integrated innovations, for example control systems that cannot be developed by one party alone.

- The specific core competencies of an individual or organisation are no longer sufficient to achieve structural innovations without external contributions.

- The customer often demands innovative products as a solution, in which case they must explicitly contribute knowledge to achieve the design of the solution.

- Rapid changes in the market require reaction times that are beyond the capacity of individual parties.

- The costs of innovation, whether or not this includes overhead costs, are too high to be borne by individual parties.

- Market uncertainty is so formidable that the risks can no longer be carried by individual parties.

- The new innovative network will give the individual participants access to new markets.

All of these reasons involve collaboration, the co-realisation of knowledge and a cooperative approach to costs and risks.

GOVERNANCE

Innovation is seen as something to be sought, not as something to be managed (Frohman 1998).

The governance of the Innovator model is fundamentally different from that of the Chameleon business model or the Foyer business model. In every structural innovation there are four areas of uncertainty that need to be managed. The first two have long been acknowledged. These are the technical uncertainty and the market uncertainty. Technical uncertainty relates to the validity of

---

Customer Insight by Innovation Point

Innovation Point LLC is a management consulting firm focused on Strategic Innovation. Customer Insight is a 'bottom-up' approach that leverages insights into the behaviours, perceptions and needs of current and potential customers by involving them as true partners in the innovation process. This non-traditional approach brings a team face-to-face with customers and consumers in order to glean fresh insights into both articulated and unarticulated problems and needs. These grass-roots insights position the team to innovate at an entirely new level. The approach is not limited to customers, but can be extended to glean insights from many other types of external stakeholders – examples include: channel partners, suppliers, employees, investors, early adopter users, media, etc. Innovation Point uses a diverse set of methods/tools, including web-based surveys and chat, focus groups and interviews, Stakeholder Panels, ethnographic research and so on, to create a deeper understanding of a company's external stakeholders at a level well beyond the articulated, and then translates this understanding into opportunities for breakthrough innovation.

(www.innovation-point.com/index.htm)

the underlying academic knowledge, the issue of whether the technology in question will work or not, the technical specifications and issues of scalability. Market uncertainties relate to customer wishes and needs, existing or latent forms of interaction between customers and potential products or services; methods of sale and distribution. The other two sources of uncertainty concern the organisation and its resources. They are more often the cause of stagnation in innovation than the first two (Leifer et al. 2000). Organisational uncertainty relates to, inter alia, the capacities of those involved in the innovation, relationship management, the ability to deal with changing levels of management support, the scale of resistance from established interests within the current business model and the likelihood of victory over a short-term focus. Financing will also demand much attention and effort. You need to unravel the requirement for financing and the sources that are available, appropriate partners and how the financing partnerships can be managed as effectively as possible. Leifer et al. (2000) contend that finding solutions to these uncertainties is of paramount importance for the management of radical innovations.

The solutions which you select for the coordination of the network depend on how the Innovator organisation is structured. The Innovator model can be considered as a continuum, of which one extreme is a fully self-sustaining network consisting of more or less equivalent participants. At the other extreme is an organisation that manages the innovation project as far as possible within its own organisational borders. Even in this extreme case the particular organisation never has full governance, since it is invariably the case that participants from outside the organisation are involved with the innovation project in some way or other. Between these two extremes we find all kinds of mixed forms. In the following subsection we will discuss the governance of both extremes, the network and the initiating organisation. The spin-out, which we will discuss in the next section, is as an example of a mixed form.

GOVERNANCE OF THE NETWORK

An organisation can set up an Innovator organisation with other participants, or join such an organisation that is already in existence, as a participant. In the latter case they can search consciously for innovative networks to which they can make a specific contribution based on their own core competencies or their access to specific markets and/or networks. Organisations are often invited by parties within an Innovator model to join, if it becomes clear during the innovation process that there is a need for their knowledge or skills. In principle the Innovator organisation is a project organisation that needs to be coordinated as such. However, as the parties have different backgrounds (and consequently often several interests), it is essential to create clarity from the outset. Distinct agreements need to be established covering the control of the network. It must be clear to all parties how decision-making will proceed and who is in control of what. Since in most situations involving the Innovator organisation as an independent network there is no single dominant party, control is more or less equally distributed among participants. In practice, however, the party that advanced the idea for the innovation will usually play a relatively salient role. An essential element in any agreement is the basis on which returns on results will be allocated. These methods of allocation should be reviewed and refined on a regular basis. It is also important that there exists tangible proof, open to all, of each participant's contributions to the results of the collaborative process. An important part of the collaboration is the acknowledgement and confirmation of both individual and common domain. The Innovator organisation needs to invest not only in businesslike relations, but also in the social conditions that promote the cooperation and thereby innovation (Miles et al. 2000).

GOVERNANCE OF INTERNAL INNOVATOR

The organisation that wishes to remain predominantly in control of the innovation needs to devote extensive thought to the question of how the innovative activities fit within its existing structure.

One of the solutions of managing uncertainties is the realisation of a 'hub' in the organisation. Leifer et al. (2000) in this regard speak of a 'natural home-base' for the key players in radical innovations; the people with the ideas, those providing venture capital, the members of project appraisal and supervising committees, and business entrepreneurs with experience of highly innovative business. A hub is a focal point for innovation; a competence centre where learning experiences around innovation are collected and distributed. A hub for radical innovation can aid in the supervision and stimulation of projects by reducing uncertainty without enforcing the bureaucracy. Hubs are 'centres

---

IBM Creates Flying Academic Brigade

IBM has formed an 'On Demand Innovation Services' division, that supports other components of the computer company with scientific knowledge. This is reported by The Wall Street Journal. On Demand Innovation Services consists of 200 R&D-researchers. They will offer their scientific knowledge in the fields of mathematics, artificial intelligence and other fields directly to IBM and its customers. Applications include the optimisation of logistics and internal communication of those customers.

of excellence' on topics such as financing, personnel, advice, facilities and the law. Through the hub, experts and mentors can help those involved with the innovation gain insight into the nature of the life cycle of innovation, and into ways to reduce uncertainties. Figure 5.6 displays the relation of the hub to the organisation and the participants.

In the hub structure (Figure 5.6), however, tension between the new organisation and the established order remains a problem. A solution for this is often found in a more independent organisational structure, such as a spin-out.

SPIN-OUT MANAGEMENT

Many organisations these days manage innovation through spin-outs. The spin-out is given the space to set up an Innovator organisation with other participants outside the original company. This may also be called a 'greenfield operation', to emphasise the start-up from 'ground zero', as far as rules and procedures go (Jagersma et al. 2001).

> *Dell Computers originated in the United States of America and has been prominent on the international market for several years now. Dell Ventures, one of the pivotal elements within Dell, specializes in constructing spin-outs. New, strategic investments that are vital for the core activities are set up through Dell Ventures and subsequently*

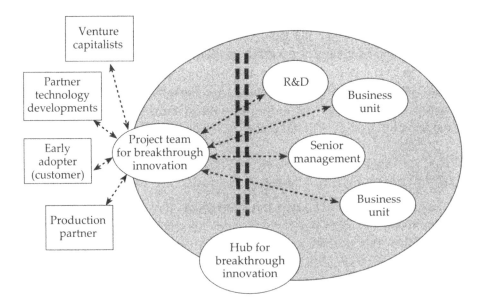

Figure 5.6   **Hub with organisation and participants**

positioned within the Dell organisation. Dell Ventures attempts to continuously rejuvenate Dell Computers Corp. by means of existing and new initiatives. The spin-outs are designed to exploit new technologies, products, and markets. A spin-out is not necessarily required to introduce a revolutionary innovation. They may also be used to develop current technologies, concepts, products, and customer contacts to higher levels. Dell uses the positive IRR (Internal Rate of Return) of spin-offs as a major indicator for financing new spin-outs. Thus 'older' spin-outs finance the 'younger' spin-outs. Spin-outs, in the context of this strategy, cannot be unprofitable for too lengthy a period of time (Jagersma et al. 2001).

To give the innovation a chance for success, the control of the organisation is not in the hands of the management of just one of the participants, but rather in the hands of a team or a separate network organisation to which considerable operational freedom is granted. In this kind of collaboration most decisions are made by mutual agreement. Many organisations work on the basis of an internal organisation that is not suitable for innovation. In traditional organisations, efficiency and (direct) profitability rather than innovation play a central role. Separating a new or existing organisational component (the spin-out) from the holding organisation allows the spin-out to focus solely on the development of new products or services. Access Point, is a case in point.

Spin-out organisations have two primary goals. In the first place spin-out management entails reduced risks: the spin-out operates closer to the market.

Innovation in the Life Sciences

A lot of money is needed for research and innovation in the Life Sciences. In large, inert and traditional hierarchical organisations, there is often no space for work on structural innovation. The Dutch department of Economic Affairs has acknowledged this fact and has formulated an 'Action Plan for Life Sciences'. From this an organisation emerged, BioPartner, that aspires to promote entrepreneurship in biotechnology, by means of initiatives, coaching, guidance, and so forth. Scientists are granted freedom to develop their ideas, unconstrained by the rules and procedures of a large organisation. It has become clear that successful start-ups are soon annexed by large biotech or pharmaceutical companies. Large companies thereby 'purchase' innovation that they themselves can no longer realise independently within of their own organisation.

Since the development of new products or services (solutions) is fraught with risks, the management of these risks and uncertainty is easier in a small flexible organisation. Second, spin-out management is designed to minimise internal hierarchy and bureaucracy. This, in turn, should increase the effectiveness of the parent organisation. The idea underlying spin-out management is that it overcomes two problems simultaneously; namely the bureaucracy and inertia of large(r) enterprises, and the lack of resources of small ones.

Spin-out management can thus function as a driving force of expansion.

It isn't all plain sailing. There are various problems inherent to spin-out management as well. The lack of a commitment to the original holding organisation and the sometimes strained business relations with the holding organisation are both potential problem areas.

> It is very difficult for a company whose cost structure is tailored to compete on high-end markets to be profitable in low-end markets as well. The only viable way to address this is to create an independent organisation, a sanctioned 'skunk works,' if you will, with a cost structure honed to achieve profitability at the low margins characteristic of most disruptive technologies. (Christensen 1997)

VIRTUAL TEAMS AND VIRTUAL COMMUNITIES

> The most famous virtual team created the Internet more than 25 years ago (Lipnack and Stamps 2000).

The previous section focused on the management of the Innovator organisation. One of the main design principles of the Innovator is that a large proportion of the activities occur in (virtual) teams and virtual communities. Virtual communities are becoming increasingly important in innovation, which is why they are included in the design principles. Because the chapter on the Foyer organisation is devoted to this issue, we will not discuss virtual communities further at this stage. Working in teams, on the other hand, will be elaborated on in this section.

The team – be it virtual or not – is referred to as the principal way of organising innovation. This is because they combine various characteristics that are essential to flexible operation. Team autonomy, though it differs from team to team, entails independent decision-making around priorities and allocation of people and resources. Teams allow several fields of expertise to be joined together, affording optimal knowledge sharing and knowledge creation. Furthermore, they allow the organisation to integrate the responsibility for a number of activities, ranging from the development of a concept to its application. Because of these characteristics, the team is able to react flexibly to changes within the market and the technology. Innovative teams can be granted a fair degree of freedom to involve participants autonomously in the innovation process.

> *The organisation with a favourable climate for innovation is one that provides the context for people to collaborate in groups, teams, divisions and departments without boundaries or fear. And since innovation is really a process of problem-solving, this informal networking cannot be limited only to internal sources. Research of 11 breakthrough innovation projects shows that informal networks were critical in all of these projects. The networks consisted of the Research & Development community, business units, customers, suppliers and governmental agencies (Tucker 2001).*

An innovative team may consist of people working together on the same site. The opportunities created by IT and communications technology also allow team working amongst people who are geographically separate. In the latter case, if the collaboration takes place with the aid of digital connections, one speaks of 'virtual teams'. It is important to understand that virtual teamwork still primarily revolves around people as opposed to technology. Moreover, the processes that are catalyst to innovation need to be carefully mapped and the communication lines with the participants must be well thought out. Lastly, keep in mind that the same pitfalls faced by 'regular' teams are faced by virtual teams, with one extra team 'killer': a disproportional focus on the technology (Lipnack and Stamps 2000).

PROCESSES

THE ORGANISATION OF LEARNING AND KNOWLEDGE SHARING

All three business models feature knowledge management. However, in the case of the Innovator model, knowledge sharing and the organisation of learning are the most essential components of the business model, as knowledge is the source of each innovation. New ideas and insights don't arise in isolation – they are the result of cooperation among individuals, each of whom offers knowledge but who learn from each other during the collaboration.

The Innovator organisation needs to balance the needs for individual learning and learning at an organisational or network level. Individual learning is important, but the organisation or network needs to profit from this learning. To achieve learning and transfer of knowledge, the Innovator organisation must eventually develop a learning culture in which knowledge sharing is encouraged and open communication established.

Learning is a combination of cognitive and social processes. Knowledge sharing and knowledge combination lead to innovations. Communication plays a central role in this process. For the creation of knowledge in the Innovator organisation, communication needs care and encouragement. Table 5.1 includes a number of measures that help develop knowledge creation in the Innovator model.

The pre-eminent principle is the creation of a free environment in both organisational structure and access to knowledge sources. Experimental learning environments depend on IT support. We will return to this issue in the next section. Virtual teams and communities are also an important condition of learning. They provide an environment in which knowledge is shared, combined and transformed into new knowledge.

Table 5.1   Measures for knowledge creation

Organisation Design	Human Factors
The use of project structures	Knowledge workers enjoy great freedom
Orientation towards new knowledge	Enhance knowledge sharing
Little (hierarchical) governance/ plenty of freedom	Stimulate new ideas
Experimental learning environments	Long-term involvement in Innovator (shared culture)
Virtual teams and communities	Stimulate change

IT AND THE INNOVATOR ORGANISATION

KNOWLEDGE MANAGEMENT AND IT

IT plays a big part in innovation; many innovations are themselves IT-products (both hard- and software). IT also plays an important role in the innovation of the business processes by which products or services are delivered. The implementation of IT in the Innovator is based on the management of knowledge in innovations.

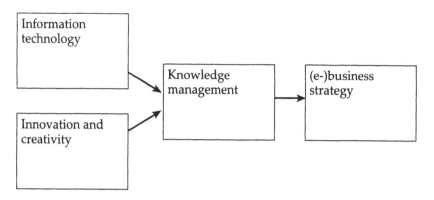

Figure 5.7 Knowledge management and strategy of Innovator

In this book, knowledge management revolves around the critical questions of the adaptation, survival and the competences of organisations, confronted with increasing structural changes within their environments. Knowledge management involves organisational processes that aim for a synergy on the one hand of the creative and innovative capacities of people and on the other the communication and learning opportunities provided by information and communication technology.

DESIGN PRINCIPLES AND IT

The opportunities provided by information and communication technology are illustrated in Figure 5.8 within the design principles of the Innovator model.

> *Software is a great enabler to innovation with extraordinary potential to change the direction and focus of organizations and industries. Software can reduce innovation cycle time, enhance results, leverage value creation, identify opportunities, learn on its own, and make innovators of everyone. Software and its capabilities currently are but in a stage of infancy. Innovators will have a great opportunity to put it to use for competitive advantage and managers everywhere will have to acknowledge that it will be at the core of future developments (Quinn et al. 1996).*

COMMUNICATION

It is particularly important for the creation of knowledge in this business model that the IT is recognised as conditional to communication. Innovation takes place in teams and/or communities. The creation of knowledge occurs on the basis of a collective memory. This is not the same as a static memory; a bookcase where knowledge is stored and expanded occasionally, but rather

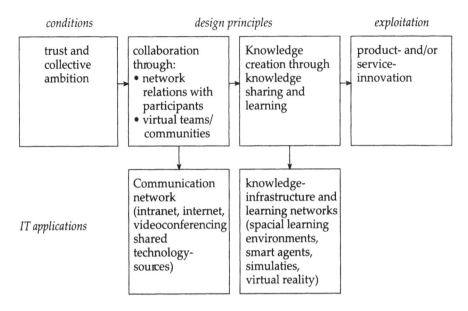

Figure 5.8   IT-opportunities in design of Innovator

a dynamic memory. In a dynamic system, knowledge is continuously both added and 'forgotten', and existing knowledge is continuously reinterpreted (Telematica Instituut 1999). In the Innovator model, participants interactively create a dynamic group memory, based on a shared understanding and a shared mental model. For this reason a shared database alone is not adequate for supporting organisational learning. IT-systems that only store knowledge contain static and often dated information that is less meaningful for innovative teams/organisations and networks. On the other hand, IT-systems that indicate who has what information and knowledge, and where, are extremely valuable. Systems of this kind have three distinct advantages:

- tThey promote the sharing of information and encourage synergy in the organisation and/or network;

- they increase awareness of who knows what i.e. what knowledge is available;

- they can help in identifying where new knowledge needs to be obtained (Telematica Instituut 1999).

The most important IT-systems, however, are the communication systems, mainly e-mail, inter- and Intranet, and groupware, because they facilitate the cooperation of people and thereby support the cooperative and learning processes in the Innovator organisation. IT should therefore not be viewed as a technology but as a communication network (Amidon 1997).

Distance-spanning communications tools open up vast new fertile grounds for 'working together at a distance.' For the first time since nomads moved into towns, work is diffusing rather than concentrating as we move from predominantly industrial to informational products and services. In all industries and sectors, people are working across space and time (Lipnack and Stamps 2000).

LEARNING APPLICATIONS

IT can provide the Innovator with a competitive advantage by catalysing the innovation cycle in the organisation in the form of a learning instrument. This exemplifies IT-applications that support and/or enable collaboration and especially experimentation in groups. IT-applications such as the Internet and groupware, enable new kinds of dialogue. The dialogue between people who learn and innovate can not only be spread over time and space; IT enables storage of conversations, fast navigation, and connections between previous conversations and other constructed knowledge. IT provides time for reflection and access to previous dialogues or other knowledge. This is why a new kind of conversation has become possible that is better suited for the depth and development of thought in a community.

Too much attention is often placed on decreasing the cost of design steps and shortening internal process times in the innovation cycle rather than focusing on the critical internal learning and value creation processes that software facilitates. Both are essential for effective innovation in today's hypercompetitive world (Quinn et al. 1996).

Amidon (1997) describes the example of Steelcase, where knowledge infrastructures are organised, which enable everybody to learn from each other. In early experiments, various IT-applications have been implemented, such as 'spatial learning environments' with 'information persistence', bulletin boards, audiovisual media, smart agents, simulations, visualisations and virtual reality applications. Depending on the situation and type of innovation to which it aspires, the Innovator organisation may make a choice from a large range of off-the-shelf and bespoke IT applications.

ROLE OF THE INTERNET

The Internet clearly takes a special place within the category of communication systems. It is not only the forum on which virtual communities are able to share their knowledge, but also the place where innovations may begin. There are indications that the worldwide information infrastructure of the Internet might in fact be a worldwide innovation infrastructure, where good ideas travel the world from the point where they arise to the point where they are needed.

ROLE OF THE (IT-)MANAGER

With the emphasis on knowledge creation and innovation, the role of the IT-manager has changed drastically. In some American companies the former Chief Information Officers now refer to their positions as 'Chief Innovation Officers' to indicate that information management principally concerns management of the knowledge infrastructure. Fortunately, the abbreviation remains unchanged. But the expanding role of IT in innovation requires changes in a wider area than simply IT-management. How you manage the participants in the Innovator organisation includes the role and application of IT in supporting innovation. The following list provides a number of questions that managers might ask themselves to assess their situation.

QUESTIONS FOR MANAGERS ABOUT IT AND INNOVATION:

- How can I reach and involve my (potential) customers and partners with my innovation, using IT and the Internet?

- How can I shape the communication so as to enable cooperation with partners/customers?

- Who should get access to what information?

- How can IT support learning and knowledge sharing in the network?

- How can I react to increasingly complex demands, made by a rapidly expanding worldwide customer base?

- How can IT support me in the search for the process for which customers desire a solution?

- What sort of virtual communities may help me in my search?

When combined with software's capacity to learn on its own, create new solutions, deal with inordinate complexities, shorten cycle times, lower costs, diminish risks and uniquely enhance customer value, effective software management has now become the key to effective innovation for any company or institution. Innovators who recognise this fact will have a genuine competitive advantage. Managers who ignore this caveat do so at their companies' peril (Quinn et al. 1996).

CONCLUSIONS

Innovation in most cases is a combination of existing technologies, ideas, knowledge and resources. Growing connectivity of people and organisations is accelerating both the number of innovations and the rate at which they occur. Organisations and networks are active in their search for innovations. Customers in turn are constantly looking for new technologies and solutions to support their own business processes. This is why the innovative business model will be, and remains, an attractive solution for many organisations and individuals. Knowledge management plays a pre-eminent role in innovations. The management of knowledge takes a different shape in the Innovator model when compared to the Chameleon and Foyer models because of the specific knowledge-intensive nature of this business model. IT takes an important place because of the opportunities the applications provide for the creation of knowledge and the support of learning. The main task laid out for management lies in the area of building and strengthening relationships in the networks and communities within which the organisation operates.

CHAPTER 6

The Foyer Model

Since the 1990s, the Internet has acquired a prominent role in organisations and in society as a whole. One of the pre-eminent aspects of the Internet is that it has united like-minded people who wish to communicate about the diverse subjects. A large number of 'virtual communities' have rapidly become established. Aside from communities that are spontaneously organised by the participants themselves, communities are also being consciously created by organisations. By joining with clients in the form of a community, an organisation gains a unique image of the opinions, wishes and knowledge of clients. The Foyer business model represents a virtual community. This business model is characterised by authenticity, shared identity and a personal relationship between the participants.

The Community Centre is Open Already!

Purchasing a house on a newly built estate often occurs more than a year before the actual move-in is possible. A whole estate with hundreds of people is thus elevated within a single year.

The future occupants have a common interest, namely the development of this new estate. Dutch Project Developer Amstelland has anticipated this fact and has created virtual communities for two estates in the Netherlands (in the cities of Dordrecht and Nijmegen).

The virtual community is set up according to the people's interests in their new living environment. Every occupant of the new estate is assigned a personal e-mail address and a personal homepage. The first encounter with the neighbours – who presently may reside hundreds of miles way – can take place virtually. The children as well can communicate with their peers and discuss hobbies with future friends. The community provides ample space for the exchange of thoughts and ideas. Depending on the phase the construction is in, the discussions change. For instance, in the early phases the discussions focus on pricing of optional expansions or simplifications, optional alternative kitchens that are offered by the Project Developer, or even the street names. Later in the process the discussion shifts towards the colours chosen to paint the house, the lay-out of gardens, the design of streets or the interior design of the houses. In each phase the project developer can place advertisements and make offers to the community for companies that provide products/ services that are appropriate to the current phase.

The responsibility to be a webmaster of the site is left to the future occupants from the start. Experience has shown that this is a critical aspect. In one of the two aforementioned estates, the role of webmaster of the website is fulfilled by two reporters Their communication skills stimulates others to actively engage as well.

Future occupants like to take pictures of their house under construction. A picture of the foundations, the first stone, the flag up high... For someone who lives in Groningen (high up north in the Netherlands) who will move to Nijmegen (more central) the journey is rather formidable if undertaken for a mere picture. Future occupants can post pictures on the photo-album themselves, but the Project Developer also posts pictures in the virtual environment. The Project Developer has placed two webcams in the new districts for the duration of construction, so that future occupants can take a glimpse at their new neighbourhood whenever they want, 24/7.

The Project Developer posts a weekly poll in the virtual community. Sentiments about a dubious matter can thus be gauged. For example, one poll concerned an unreasonable price for the control panel of the heating system (future occupants had found the same control panel for nearly half the price at a local store). This enables the Project Developer to take into account the opinions of future occupants and to accommodate them appropriately.

The virtual community centre is the locus of vigorous chatting activity. At some point chatters even arranged meetings. 'Hey neighbour, are you coming to the community centre tomorrow? It's already open!'

(Source: presentation H. Schuttenbeld, director Madocke, at the symposium 'Virtual Communities', Leiden, June 12th 2001)

INTRODUCTION

Of the three business models discussed in this book, the Foyer business model is the one that ventures furthest from traditional ways of doing business. The Chameleon model involves a more or less traditional way of organising in which the possibilities afforded by IT are exploited to the best effect. In the Innovator model an organisation no longer rules supreme but will need to adapt itself as part of the network. Functioning in networks is, however, not wholly unfamiliar to organisations. And, the Innovator model is designed and governed in a way that is familiar to most businesses. For instance, there is a form of management and the participants primarily use agreements as a means of controlling their collaboration. In the Foyer business model, on the other hand, one can genuinely speak of a revolution. A business model that is organised by the participants and where an organisation can only join or act as a facilitator, is a frightening idea for many managers.

> *What can a group of loosely organized users accomplish without product developers, factories and marketing departments? More than most manufacturers would care to admit, points out von Hippel, who is a professor at the MIT Sloan School of Management. Aided by the Internet to support collaboration and distribution, the power and pervasiveness of such communities could become enormously amplified (von Hippel 2001).*

The energy that emanates from a group of people who share an interest, communicate and believe in one goal, is very appropriate for a business model. The basis for communication in a field of shared interest suggests security, fondness, warmth and light. All these are attributes most closely associated with a hearth-fire: hence the name Foyer.

The fact that the Foyer model currently enjoys surging popularity stems not only from the fact that the Internet now enables such communities. The Foyer model fits today's spirit of the age, since it partly appeals to ideas associated with the 'emotion economy' or 'experience economy' (Pine and Gilmore 1999). A hallmark of the emotion economy is the increasing importance of brand

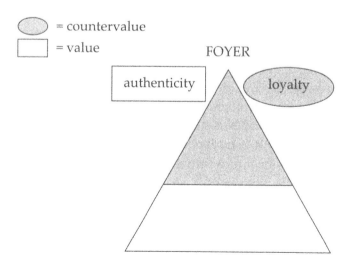

Figure 6.1   Business model Foyer

names focused on 'lifestyle' attributes and on 'customer communities'. Pine and Gilmore, in the 'experience economy', emphasise experience as the next step in the line-up of resources – products – services. Such developments force individuals and organisations to confront a number of fundamental questions surrounding business and how it is conducted. This, in turn, leads to new strategic routes, such as the Foyer business model.

In the following section, we discuss differences and similarities between virtual communities and the Foyer business model. We will discuss also how an individual or organisation may make use of the Foyer as a business model. And we will describe, from a strategic perspective, the value exchange that may take place in the Foyer model. The chapter includes a focus on the way communication with the market occurs. (This is where the Foyer differs fundamentally from the Chameleon model and the Innovator model). We also present the principles that play a role in the design of a Foyer. Without IT, and the Internet in particular, the Foyer business model is unworkable.

VIRTUAL COMMUNITIES AND FOYERS

In recent years virtual communities have regularly been the focus of articles and books, and all sorts of definitions and descriptions have surfaced (Melger 2001). The Foyer business model is always a virtual community, but not all virtual communities can be classified as this business model.

DEFINITION OF THE VIRTUAL COMMUNITY

A virtual community is a self-organising group of people that engage together in activities over the Internet. The people are part of the virtual community because they share a common interest in the subject. The community is the vehicle for an exchange of information about the subject, a sharing of knowledge or of a service that the members wish to provide to one other in the context of their shared interest. This description is valid for any type of virtual community. The main distinguishing factors between virtual communities are the different interests and the different goals for which the participants strive. These goals have an effect on the culture of a virtual community, as well as on the way the participants communicate with and relate to one other. A virtual community has a very open nature; participants decide how the community will operate. The social interaction between participants is supported and facilitated by information and communication technology. IT is the platform for a communal culture.

GENERATING REVENUES: THE FOYER

It was discovered fairly quickly following the emergence of the first virtual communities, that these communities could generate value. Organisations found that a virtual community could function as a powerful tool for generating business. By appealing to the feelings of shared identity and loyalty, participating organisations were able to attract clients, offer complementary products and services, communicate more efficiently, but also to innovate by providing the catalyst for a new community involving participants of most interest to them.

Obviously not all virtual communities are suitable and/or willing to offer business advantages to organisations. That is why not all communities can be classified as the Foyer business model. The difference between the term virtual community in general and the Foyer lies in the generation of activities that give rise to revenues for one or more of the participants. These may be revenues with commercial (profit-) goals, but also revenues with more idealistic goals. An example of the latter is the Down Syndrome Online Advocacy Group. This is a virtual community that may be classified as the Foyer business model.

ROLES IN THE FOYER MODEL

There are three roles in the Foyer model: the facilitator, the commercial participant and the non-commercial participant.

Uniting the Like-minded in DSOAG

The Down Syndrome Online Advocacy Group (DSOAG) aspires to form a platform for parents that have children with the Down Syndrome and for researchers that occupy themselves with this condition. DSOAG thus tries to unite the two groups, so that they may understand better the needs and wishes of one another. Their services include the following:

- support of the interaction between researchers and parents with afflicted children;
- provision of information for those interested in how to acquire funds from the American government, and how these funds are allocated;
- access to an Internet portal with various links to other websites that provide information about this condition. (Preece 2000)

The Foyer for this community is shaped by offering members and visitors insights and the option of making donations to researchers through legal organisations.

The Facilitator

If no appropriate community already exists, organisations may start a Foyer alone or with partners. These organisation(s) can then be considered as the owner(s) of the technological infrastructure. The people or organisations that founded and technically administer the Foyer network are referred to as 'facilitators'. It should be very clear that the organisation is never to be considered as the owner of the Foyer. This would disturb the pattern of equality among participants. If participants start to feel as if they or the community as a whole are being exploited solely for commercial ends, the community is sure to collapse. Organisations will need to invest considerable effort into the community to stimulate relationship-building and the development of the shared identity. At the same time, however, this does create the opportunity to influence the virtual community itself, and to shape – at least partially – the Foyer model to your own aspirations.

The Commercial participant

If the virtual community already exists, a person or organisation may join in order to generate long term revenues. However, it is possible that the community was started by another organisation. This organisation has probably already been exercising its influence on the operation and/or the design of the Foyer model, which might mean that it will not allow third parties to engage in certain activities within the community, or that third parties are limited in this regard. Given the dynamics of the virtual community and the strength of the Foyer business model, it is more likely that certain constraints apply, rather than that access is denied. After all, the total value of a virtual community consists of all the values that the community as a whole can offer its individual participants. New member organisations can add new value to the community and increase the value for the existing participants. An organisation that joins an existing virtual community will, however, often have to conform to the set rules of the community.

The Non-commercial participant

The third and most important role in the model is played by the participants who join the community out of personal interest. They do not aspire to make money, but find a community in the network, in which they can exchange knowledge and information about their field of interest, and build relations with like-minded people. It is thanks to these participants that the sense of security, warmth and community spirit arise: the basis of the Foyer model.

STRATEGY

Because the Foyer model does not represent a business organisation, but a community of people who share an interest, there is no one strategy behind the Foyer model. However, the various participants each engage in the community with their own strategy, their own specific desired value(s) and willingness to offer reciprocal value(s).

VALUES

The most important value each Foyer community offers the participant/client is the feeling of authenticity and shared identity, of the sharing of values and norms, in short, of 'belonging'. Authenticity implies that the organisation does not offer a mere illusion of a shared identity, simply for the purposes of marketing idea, but that there is a real sense of community.

The Digital Lonely Planet

Lonely Planet is well-known among travellers and backpackers. The travel guides and the website aim to help the individual traveller with sights to see, tourist information and routes, but especially with practically useful informational such as city maps, hotel descriptions (quality, summary of rooms, location, price, etc.), tips for restaurants, transportation (departure schedules, prices, alternatives), and so on. Since 2005, a new travel community has been in existence, which has followed and developed the kind of community created by the Lonely Planet, namely World66 (www.world66.com). It is based on Wikipedia (www.wikipedia.org), where content is created from articles, pictures, tips, and so forth, added by users themselves to the site.

Another value that the Foyer community offers its participants is access to knowledge and information. There is a sense of mutual solidarity which allows the participants to retrieve and/or provide answers to questions that might arise in the field of interest. This in turn may lead to the sharing of experiences that are not focused on knowledge exchange, but on social well-being, as in the example of The Well. This process can create and maintain the value of social relations.

In a Foyer model, additional knowledge and information about specific products and services may be offered. The participant gains a better perspective on the supply of products and services, but also on potential cooperative partners in the case of a commercial venture.

The WELL

The Whole Earth 'Lectronic Link' (WELL) is one of the oldest virtual communities in existence and to many provides a place where they may feel at home. Although the WELL was originally a digital environment where the writers and readers of the Whole Earth Review entered into debate, the WELL has grown into a colourful community where intelligent, intense, but also emotional discussions take place. Many authors have attempted to exemplify the emotional side of virtual communities by means of the WELL. Rheingold, for example, describes extensively his personal experiences in the 'parenting conference', which is a sub-community in the WELL. Many parents come together in this sub-community to share the joys, and hardships, inherent to parenthood. For instance, Rheingold gives an intricate account of how the sub-community actually became a platform for emotional support, for a family that had a child diagnosed with leukaemia.

(Rheingold 1993).

Tweakers.net

Tweakers.net is one of the larger Dutch virtual communities in the field of hardware and software. Since September 1998, the site has mainly published hardware reviews, but it has slowly expanded to become a fully interactive site. Now it provides access to news, hardware and software reviews, a 'price watch', a 'shop survey', supply and demand, a forum, and game servers for 'Unreal', 'Quake', and 'Half-life'. What makes tweakers.net a real virtual community is the fact that all the offered components are provided with content, not only by the organisation behind the community, but also by visitors and companies. This leads to an effective and efficient exchange of information.

The participant will not only be offered knowledge and information by the Foyer community, the Foyer may also offer services and products. A participant is thus more able to meet their needs through the membership. This is true for both commercial and non-commercial participants.

Parties who wish to promote mutual collaboration through the community may also participate in the Foyer network. This is usually the case when commercial participants are involved. This approach enables the participant to gain access to, and insight into, the various competences that are represented in the network.

The last value offered by the model is its range. Virtual communities cross the boundaries of a physical community; boundaries that were previously fixed in time and place. Thanks to the Internet these boundaries are no longer constraints. In principle, everyone around the world with a similar interest can participate. This is an important value the Foyer model offers all three of the kinds of participants. It is important to the non-commercial participants because it allows them to ask questions about their field of interest to a much wider audience than was previously possible. This has turned out to be a particularly important value in networks that focus on specific diseases. The community of the DSOAG, which has already been described, is a good example. For both the commercial participants and the facilitator it offers them a much greater range for topics on which they offer information, or for selling their products or services, than they would have without the community.

RECIPROCAL VALUES IN THE FOYER

In exchange for the values they receive, participants offer their loyalty to the community. This is an extremely relevant reciprocal value. Loyalty is of great significance to all participants, but is particularly important to the commercial participants and the facilitator. After all, when an organisation provides a service to the community and to individual participants as a commercial participant, this has the potential to develop into a powerful mutual relation. The expression of this relationship in the community can lead to improved reputation for that particular organisation, which in turn may lead to a better competitive position in the market. This is often referred to by the term 'branding' and is a fact that holds true for both the commercial participants and the facilitator.

Aside from, or rather thanks to, this loyalty and the activities that are developed in the community, other reciprocal values can be created that may be beneficial to all. For example, the Foyer model offers potential insights into the market. Participants will display a certain kind of behaviour and express opinions and needs concerning products and services. By participating in the network and observing the participants, commercial participants may gain valuable information about the market.

Through the bond that is forged with the participants, organisations (both commercial and facilitators) are enabled to find out about their products, services, and other matters.

Myspace

Myspace is an online community, a kind of city on the Internet. It is a community where young like-minded people meet. An important shared interest of young people is music. In the United States and England, Myspace is of paramount importance for music bands. If a band has a lot of friends in Myspace, it will be booked without hesitation. The Arctic Monkeys was a hit on Myspace before they became famous.

SmartGirl Internette

SmartGirl Internette is a virtual community oriented towards teenage girls specifically. They find in this community a platform where they can raise for discussion all the issues that occupy their minds, uninhibitedly. These can involve news about gaming, books, magazines or films. Such newsflashes are primarily written by the teenagers themselves. They can also write and read about topics concerning sex, issues surrounding divorces, clothing, relationships and so on.

The added value for participating organisations lies in the polls, regularly filled out by the girls, on their tastes in clothing, their opinions on celebrities and so forth. Organisations can either buy this information, or post their own polls. In this way, the information in the community is exploited by the organising party (facilitator).

This feedback will also include information about the competition. Because the participants have a common interest, considerable information about the various products and services in the market is shared in the community. For a commercial participant and/or the facilitator this includes valuable information about the actions of competitors. For the non-commercial participant this covers items such as the best products and manufacturers.

A reciprocal value in the Foyer model is decreased transaction costs. Participants can be both (potential) clients, and (potential) cooperative partners and suppliers. Since participation in the Foyer provides easy access to the group, the transaction costs for all (kinds of) participants should be low. For example, it takes less time to search for the best product or the best supplier. Thanks to the sense of trust in the community and the reputation of the organisation within it, it may be easier to draw up contracts, offer guarantees and so on. The decrease in marketing costs is a specific form of decreased transaction costs and is an important reciprocal value the Foyer model can offer organisations.

This can never be guaranteed, but it is an ideal objective for an organisation wishing to keep these costs as low as possible. A Foyer network offers a way to achieve this goal. The organisation knows the community is made up of people with an interest that is related to the products or services that it is offering. This means that the offer is much more focused on the target group. Second, the organisation can exploit endorsement through various participants. After all, participants often share information amongst themselves about the quality of an organisation's products and services (Prahalad and Ramaswany 2000). Good news will spread quickly. A community is an excellent form of 'viral marketing'. Unfortunately, bad news can spread at an equal pace and can just as easily tarnish the reputation of an organisation. Figure 6.2 illustrates the possible value exchanges.

REVENUE MODEL

Sales of products or services through the community is one of the ways in which commercial participants and the facilitator can profit from the community. The facilitator has more options available. Using the technical infrastructure of the network, the facilitator can support commercial participants to ensure value exchanges proceed smoothly. For instance, different technical applications can help the commercial participant in gaining more insight into the market, by offering overviews of participant behaviour.

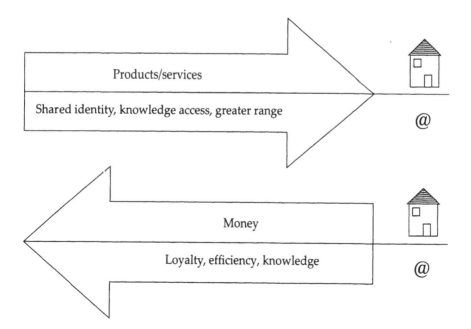

Figure 6.2 Value model Foyer

Another option is to offer to the commercial participant facilities to promote their products and services throughout the virtual community. Commercial participants can be charged for all these facilities, for instance in the form of fixed transaction costs whenever they employ the functionality offered by the network (Green 1999). Recommendation costs, otherwise referred to as 'affiliation', can also produce financial reciprocal values (Weill and Vitale 2001). Affiliation relies on the fact that a virtual community consists of a series of relationships, which can be exploited by other organisations for which they can then be charged. Variable or fixed sales commissions and advertising revenue are two potential sources of revenues for the facilitator. Variable sales commissions acknowledge the dependence of the price on factors such as the size of the order, the duration of the assignment and so on, whereas fixed sales commissions are agreed charges for a successful transaction enabled by the relationships within the Foyer. Finally, charging commercial participants for their participation, in the form of a subscription costs for example, is always an option.

MARKET COMMUNICATION

The operation and continuity of the Foyer model are wholly dependent on the efforts and willingness to cooperate of the participants. For this reason many of the value exchanges are only possible if the community consists of a group of close, devoted and active participants. Careful and continuous communication with the 'market' (the current and potential participants) is therefore especially important in this business model.

SEVERAL COMMUNICATION FLOWS

Market communication in the Foyer model revolves around the nature of the relationship with the participant and the conditions this communication needs to satisfy. In other words, it does not concern the relationship to a particular market. This is because the concept of a market is too limited, since the term usually refers only to the market of consumers. In the Foyer model, however, there are more parties than simply 'consumers'. Producers, suppliers, partners and clients can all participate. The market includes the entire group that shares the interest. As a consequence multiple communication flows are required. A different message will need to be sent to each different target group, because each looks for different values from the community. It is the facilitator's task to manage these various communication flows. The facilitator will need to ensure that producers know what to expect from the community, that commercial participants know how best to offer their products and services, and that non-commercial participants know which values they will encounter in the community.

The market communication thus has two goals in the Foyer model. On the one hand, the communication needs to express the purpose of the community, to reach the potential market and/or potential participants. On the other hand, the communication needs to express the goals of the parties in the community that generate income through it. These two types of communication must in no way be at odds and can assume different forms for each participating party.

DEMAND-ORIENTED MARKET COMMUNICATION

Another important aspect of the market communication in the Foyer model stems from the fact that the community is wholly 'demand-oriented'. This is a consequence of the dynamics of the virtual community. The social relations aspects ensure the bond between the participants of a virtual community. At the same time, however, this also implies that the bond can be a loose one, because the community operates virtually. As a result, there are (almost) no direct consequences for someone who decides to leave or behave in a way that is contrary to the norms and values of the community. Some authors even argue that leaving a virtual community is as easy as 'zapping' from channel to channel on the television (Fernback and Thompson 2000). As a consequence, the Foyer model must offer substantial value if it wants to keep its participants. This is only possible when the needs of the non-commercial participants are diligently heeded. In this case, you can truly say that 'the customer is king'.

METHODS OF COMMUNICATION

It is important that the facilitator and the commercial participants check carefully to what extent the business-like character of their communication harmonises with the emotional and social side of the virtual community. This involves recognising the relevant signals from the discussions by participants. Commercial participants need to assume an observing, listening and waiting role, where feedback, support and the provision of information on demand take a central place, rather than an aggressive form of promotion for products and services. On the other hand, they themselves can initiate activities, by creating a certain market need in the community. But this will not succeed through overt promotion of products or services, because it will run counter to the feelings of authenticity of the participants. The facilitator and the commercial participants will need to generate a certain experience around the product and/or service, in order to stimulate discussion about it amongst the participants. Participants will need to be encouraged to gather more information about the product or service (market need).

Failure to understand this basic tenet can result in aggressive promotion/sales activities that will deter participants. This can severely damage the reputation of the organisation responsible, but can also harm the community itself. Ryan and Whiteman (2000) discovered that advertisers believe that participants in a virtual community do not pay much attention to advertisements, because their own discussions are a much more important source of information and interest. In the Foyer model, the key task for an organisation remains to work out the best form of communication with different participants.

DESIGN OF THE FOYER: COMMUNITY CENTRAL

Figure 6.3 illustrates the design parameters and conditions of the Foyer model.

CONDITIONS FOR THE FOYER MODEL

Relational trust

Just as with the Innovator model, trust is a necessary prerequisite for the Foyer model to function and flourish. In the case of the Foyer model, this trust can be characterised as 'relational' trust, which means trust that is based on the social relationships of the participants. Relational trust can be viewed as the confidence that one party has in the nature of the collaboration with another, no matter what the eventual outcome. This is a different kind of trust than that often described in the literature, which focuses on the confidence in a good result. Relational trust therefore is more personally oriented and can greatly improve any collaboration (Jansen et al. 2002). The facilitator can establish the network in a way that enables participants to build mutual trust. For example by defining the consequences of incorrect behaviour or providing insights into the background of the participants (Melger 2001).

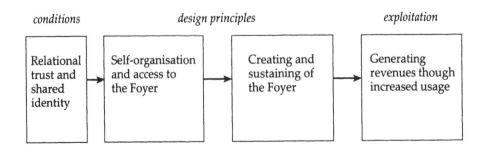

Figure 6.3   Design principles Foyer

Shared identity

Participants in the Foyer model have a clear shared identity. This means that they identify each other as belonging to the (temporary) community of which they are all part. This identity consists of persistent characteristics with which they distinguish themselves from other organisations (Kogut and Zander 1996). These characteristics become visible through the habits and rules by which the participants coordinate their behaviour and decision-making processes. People know what to expect from one another. In part it is thanks to this that problems can be solved amicably and that activities are based on the same presuppositions. Trust in each other and a shared identity form the basis for communication and knowledge-sharing in the Foyer.

DESIGN PRINCIPLES

Governance

The design of governance is an important part of an organisation. This is no simple feat in the Foyer model, because the community forms a self-organising whole. This is sometimes compared to an ecosystem that adapts independently to its environment (Hagel and Armstrong 1997; Canter and Siegel 1995). As a result, governance, as it is normally implemented in organisations (hierarchically), is not appropriate for the self-organising dynamics of the Foyer. On the other hand, groups that cooperate in order to reach a common goal and that communicate via 'computer mediated communication' (CMC), often need a leader somewhere in the system to stay motivated and successful. When this is missing there is a good chance that the group will not reach the end goal (Jarvenpaa and Leidner 1998; Kollock 1999).

CHANGING GOVERNANCE BETWEEN PARTICIPANTS

This antithesis may seem contradictory, but it is one of the reasons why the governance of a Foyer community is so complex. The label 'self-organising' does not imply that governance is wholly absent, but that this aspect is realised in a different way. An ecosystem is generally based on 'survival of the fittest'. The organism that is most adept at adapting to its environment survives and will play a dominant role in the new environment. In the Foyer network, you will encounter various participants that engage in leading roles. Usually this is based on the acknowledgement of a group of the qualities associated with particular participants. Reputation is often at the core of this process. Such a reputation can be built on the basis of the extent to which a participant applies themselves to the community or because they have the most knowledge in a particular field. These distinctions enable certain roles to be assigned to various members who then proceed to assume the responsibility for the governance. It is important to note that the participants themselves, rather than the facilitator or the commercial participants, assign these roles to each other.

ARRANGING ACCESS

An important design principle for the Foyer model is the design of 'access' to the community. When a Foyer community materialises, the value it offers can be transformed into 'relatively free access'. This means that the access is not completely free. Participants will need to register, display appropriate behaviour, apply themselves to the community and so on. This can be viewed as a form of 'etiquette'. Thus, not everyone will gain access to all facilities of the community straight away; access must be earned. This is true for both non-commercial participants and for commercial participants. The benefit of this approach for the participant is that outsiders do not enjoy the same privileges as members. It is therefore in their interest to register and make an effort for the community. In other words, membership implies both effort and added value. The advantage of this approach is that the Foyer community will be made up of motivated participants, and that the true nature of the community is protected to an extent. The facilitator is the guardian of etiquette and of the access to the Foyer network. The participants will also play an important role in this by drawing the facilitator's attention to inappropriate behaviour and by committing themselves to the etiquette.

PROCESSES

The processes within a virtual community and the Foyer model are somewhat different from the processes in the Chameleon or the Innovator models. The reason for this is that the governance is in the hands of the participants themselves. They decide what happens. This means that the processes within the community cannot be clearly defined in advance. However, there are three distinct processes: the creation, maintenance and exploitation. These are displayed in Figure 6.4.

CREATION

For the Foyer to emerge successfully, it is essential that all those who participate have or acquire a clear picture of what they want and which of their needs can be fulfilled.

Creating	Sustaining	Using
• communicate vision community and Foyer • stimulate participants by core team • dioscover needs of participants • create IT infrastructure	• sharing knowledge • activate participants • stimulate participants to engage in the organisation of Foyer • conflict handling • promote vision	• communicate vision Foyer • discover new strategic values • generating revenues by the Foyer

Figure 6.4   Process Foyer

Communicating the vision of the Foyer

The facilitator starts with a certain vision that forms the basis of the decision to facilitate a Foyer community. This community may already exist, or there may be a group of people with a shared interest who are not yet all in contact with each other. The facilitator will need to bring the idea of a common community to the attention of all potential participants, both commercial and non-commercial, and communicate the vision to them. The facilitator will need to be clear. The goal of the process is to attract as many participants as possible and to demonstrate the value of the Foyer community compared to other alternatives in the same field of interest.

Stimulation of participants for the formation of a core group

Engaged participants form the basis of a close community. The facilitator will need to start a process to attract and engage participation. This may involve virtual events, for instance a web-discussion with a prominent expert. The goal of the process is to create a small, close core group within the community that will itself draw new ideas and trends into the community.

Identification of participants' needs

Participants' needs change continuously. The community requires the means to react and adapt appropriately. The facilitator will need to engage in specific activities to track participants' needs and to act on them. For this reason the space between the participant and the facilitator becomes a central issue. The facilitator cannot coordinate the community from a distance, but will need to engage with participants. Specific activities can help in this purpose, such as opinion polls.

Establishment of the IT-infrastructure

Because the Foyer community is virtual, core IT-facilities are needed. The facilitator will need to establish how IT can best be employed to give optimal support to the participants in the network.

Maintaining the Foyer model

Once the first arrangements have been made to establish the community and a stable foundation for the network has been created, the emphasis of the process shifts from creation to maintenance.

SHARING KNOWLEDGE

The most important values of the Foyer are a feeling of belonging and the exchange of information and knowledge. These two different values are complementary. The virtual character of the Foyer means that information is the first value to be provided. At the same time, the open information exchange will be an invitation to share and develop knowledge together. This process stimulates the social sense of belonging, which in turn promotes the information and knowledge exchange. This process is displayed in Figure 6.5.

The sharing of knowledge in the Foyer network is thus an important facet for the success of the business model. This can be classified as knowledge management, where – as in the Innovator model – the emphasis is not on a careful storage of knowledge, but more on its exchange and exploitation. The difference between knowledge management in the Chameleon and the Innovator models and the Foyer model is that the knowledge management is not a conscious strategy in the Foyer community. It is a spontaneous process that is developed by the participants. Among the participants a large knowledge base lays dormant, waiting to be discovered amongst mutual contacts and the relationships that are developed. This is why the process may be compared to an exploration, in which experiences serve as sources of inspiration for further exploration, and guide the building and exploitation of knowledge.

STIMULATING PARTICIPANTS

Participants need to be stimulated and motivated, not so much to form a core group, but to keep the community alive. This is where the concept of challenge becomes relevant. Some challenge and commotion in the community may lead to a strengthening of the relations between participants. This is analogous to

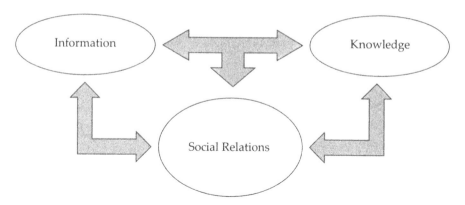

Figure 6.5 Relation between Information, Knowledge and Social Relations

politics, where extremist politicians can stir up an apathetic public through their fierce line and the successes it achieves; encouraging people to occupy themselves once more with political issues. In the Foyer model the art lies in the containment of conflicts, so that they do not escalate. Certain promotional campaigns can be set up in the community for the participants themselves to soon take over. All this is the focus of the process 'engaging of participants'.

Stimulation of the participants to assume and fulfil roles

Under the process of 'engaging of participants', we mentioned that participants should take over responsibility for activities that are set up by the facilitator as soon as possible. Participants will need to be assigned roles (in the ideal situation participants take roles by themselves) otherwise this may be subtly enabled. The facilitator can use various activities to this end. For example, debates can be organised within the community which will assign the status of expert to certain participants.

Conflict management

The facilitator together with the participants will need to define how conflicts should be handled, for example, how to revoke privileges in the case of any abuse of the facilities. The facilitator must take care not to operate as a dictator, rather as a judge, whose first task is to investigate what exactly occurred by listening to the accounts of those involved.

Disseminating the vision

Newcomers to the community may find it hard to ascertain the added value that it offers. The facilitator will need to make it clear, one way or another, what the particular community is all about and what its advantages are for potential participants. Disseminating the community vision is therefore an important aspect in supporting new members.

Usage

All participants will use the Foyer network for their own goals. These may range from visits to the community for social contact, through to participation in the community to generate revenues.

INFORMATION AND COMMUNICATION TECHNOLOGY

The particularity of the Foyer business model is that the IT-infrastructure is actually a prerequisite for the community to exist. In this sense, IT, and especially the Internet, is the 'enabler' of the model. This means that all participants must carefully consider whether or not their needs can be met through existing IT-infrastructure. In the start-up phase, the facilitator will need to check whether the basic IT functionality and the basic information needs of the participants have been established and are met. It is also of importance to have a flexible infrastructure. And you need to verify that the workings of the IT-infrastructure are self-evident for the community. Complex navigation and over-elaborate user interfaces are undesirable. Trustworthiness and safety are also important

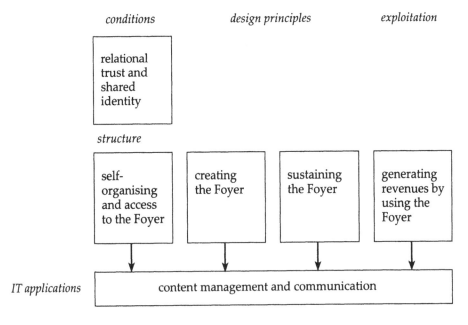

Figure 6.6   Design principles and IT Foyer

aspects. As the content of communication in the community will be primarily digital, content management systems are particularly useful for managing the information.

CONTENT MANAGEMENT

Given the virtual character of the community and the many potential interactions among participants, a great deal of information and knowledge may be exchanged in various ways. For the facilitator and commercial participants it is important to exploit appropriate information and knowledge for business objectives. The sheer quantity of content, however, makes it difficult to manage. Content management is an approach that benefits from some of the latest IT developments. Various IT-applications enable the reuse of content, but also the filtering and modification of information for business objectives. For instance, new techniques have made it possible to filter specific information from chat-groups or bulletin boards, and to show it in aggregated form on the website. It is important for the facilitator to provide such content management facilities for the (commercial) participants.

IT for communication

Communication is the critical success factor in the Foyer model. For this reason IT-applications that promote communication and that facilitate a search for contacts and/or information will be important. Search systems, systems for the support of navigation and intelligent agents are examples of these applications.

IT for transaction processing systems and systems for cooperation

Commercial participants within the Foyer model must ensure a seamless connection of the internal IT within their organisation in the areas of transaction processing and the collaboration with those partners involved in the distribution of products or services or information about them.

CONCLUSIONS

The primary characteristic of the Foyer business model is the self-organising capacity of its participants. This means that you need to be reticent when it comes to influencing the Foyer community for commercial purposes. This influence runs the risk of upsetting or destroying the community. The starting point is the power that emanates from people who have gathered around a particular field of interest, and who communicate and share the faith in a similar goal.

Organisations that wish to generate revenues from the Foyer community will need to create win-win situations. Participants must be willing to voluntarily engage in activities on behalf of the organisation (commercial participant/ facilitator). These may be diverse, such as the provision of information and the autonomous organisation of meetings. If the participants themselves can see the relevance of these activities and are willing to assume responsibility for their organisation, then there is a good chance that the participants or 'customers' will not feel exploited by a commercial objective. The success of the Foyer model depends on adequate and focused attention to the main processes which ensure its viability. The focus of commercial organisations should lie in enabling participants to communicate, participate and exchange thoughts and ideas. Only then will added value emerge for participants and they will make an energetic effort to ensure the continued existence of the Foyer community.

CHAPTER 7

Business Dynamics

In this age of rapid developments in information and communication technology and the ways in which organisations react to them, the issue of business dynamics is highly relevant. Not going forward means losing ground, to the extent that you can speak of the 'Red Queen-effect' (Volberda 1998). The Red Queen is a character in 'Alice in Wonderland', who decrees that characters need to run in order to stay in place (and to avoid going backwards).

Organisations display certain dynamics. The choice of a particular business model is temporary in most cases. Organisations will continuously need to be open to new developments and transitions to other business models. This chapter is about why and how organisations shift from one type of business model to another and how they may adopt possible combinations of two or more types of business models. The most important element is expectations for the future. What type of business model is going to 'shine' and what can organisations expect?

Organisations have now been routinely installing digital equipment, company software and/or communication facilities for years. But in order to really use these effectively, businesses will need to restructure not only their activities, but their entire organisation. Nobody yet knows how this ought to proceed exactly. Companies don't know what the 'right' organisations will look like and are confronted with the realistic possibility that any reorganisation will soon be outdated by new technologies. Even if organisations would know how the new forms would look, then still they would need to pay for the costs of changing the old structures. Much of the technology has long been available, but its implementation requires a slow process of learning and investments. In principle such a process of annihilating old structures and the slow adoption of IT through all American industrial branches has taken place during the nineties of the previous century. This is the exact reason for virtually all substantial productivity profits in this decade. Two recent studies show that this process continues, and that even after the crash the productivity profits have scarcely decreased. The reason for this is simple. Crash or no crash, the prices of IT continue to decline and companies continue to profit from this by purchasing the new technology and adopting their methods to it. This is healthy but not yet sufficient. The real profits follow when the new technology begins to adapt to the businesses. The information revolution is not significantly different from other technological revolutions. The Internet has seen the phases of enormous growth and the crash, and there is no reason to assume that the information revolution will follow a different path than previous revolutions. Eventually this will lead to the full adaptation of the technology. That has always occurred up to this point. But it does mean that the technology is easy to apply for the user and that companies will reshape themselves in order to implement the technology. This will gradually take place in the next 10 to 20 years.

(Arthur 2002)

INTRODUCTION

The three business model types that are described in this book can be regarded as extremes of a triangle. A business model indicates the right way to do business at a particular point in time. This means that the choice an organisation makes of where to be on the triangle is less important than the choice of partners and clients, with whom to build a network. The focus is no longer on the individual organisation, as in more traditional business models. This implies that within an organisation different business units may also opt for different business models. After all, separate units operate autonomously. Royal Philips Electronics NV is aware of the potential for such differentiation. During a meeting on securing the Internet in the organisation, the Philips Team concluded that differentiation and integration go hand in hand.

A second point of interest is the fact that every type of business model represents an ideal type, to which an effective combination of strategy, design and IT belongs. An ideal type is formed from characteristics and elements of the given phenomena but it is not meant to correspond to all of the characteristics of any one particular case. Although in reality such ideal types (virtually) never occur, the theoretical model provides a convenient starting point for consistent reflection on the business in which you find (or want to find) yourself and the consequences of this for your design and your IT. The central question that presents itself, is whether or not a combination of the three described business model types is a better solution than any single model.

Securing the Internet within Philips Electronics NV

We lay the responsibility for all activities primarily with the business. In this way new activities automatically receive a strong focus. Naturally, for every business unit the Internet implementation can differ. At the same time we realise that we may miss an opportunity if we do not adopt a more holistic perspective towards the consumer. To address this issue we have already developed the first Philips-wide consumer mental models. These models describe how consumers make purchase decisions and brand choices and perceive benefits. Philips is convinced that, as Internet implementation is designed increasingly as a loyalty-channel, Internet-related cross-connections between the business units will emerge.

(De Wilde and Van Brenk 2002)

In this chapter we discuss the direction that business transformation is likely to take, for each of the business models in turn. In each of these sections we include an interview with an expert commentator and a forecast about the application of the relevant business models.

DYNAMICS OF THE CHAMELEON

In Chapter 4 we concluded that, at the moment, the Chameleon is the business model that is most frequently adopted, whole or in part, by a large number of organisations. Nonetheless, in practice we find experimentation; combinations of the Chameleon model with components of the other two types, driven by the need for customer involvement or for innovations. This section looks at combinations of the Chameleon model with each of the other models.

CHAMELEON–FOYER

In the Chameleon business model it is the organisation that determines the supply of products and services. Clients are given a choice of a limited number of components, that enable a product or service to meet their demands better. Nonetheless, in a large number of Chameleon organisations, a trend of trying to involve the clients with the products or services and with the production process is visible. More and more companies join existing virtual communities or start up new ones in order to engage the client in product or service improvements. Where clients have specific questions concerning the product or service the organisation can answer these, but the answer may just as likely be supplied by other users that have encountered similar problems before, and have found adequate solutions. The moment that customers begin to engage actively in certain communities and a feeling of shared identity starts to emerge, there is a transition from the Chameleon towards the Foyer model. For example, designers in Microsoft environments extensively debate the possibilities of Microsoft Development tools, ask each other questions, and solve each other's problems. The organisation (Microsoft) is dominantly present in the virtual community. In fact, ownership of the community was deemed so important at one point that Microsoft designed the community in order to revive a Newsgroup, which had once been founded independently of the company.

When the sense of community becomes so great that a relationship with the initial organisation and/or their products seems to have vanished or when the members experience the interference or governance of the organisation as a limiting factor, the community may choose to deploy its activities in a new and different way. A pure version of the Foyer business model then becomes the natural next step.

CHAMELEON–INNOVATOR

A Chameleon organisation sells personalised products/services. The modular structure of the product/service enables the organisation to adopt this strategy. This means that certain combinations of components together form a product/ service. The composition of these components may vary over time and new components may be added. This can be classified as an incremental innovation, since the product is improved, but there is not actually a new product. Improvements of existing components can also be considered incremental innovations. These incremental innovations are often initiated by wishes or needs of clients. Organisations with a Chameleon business model spend substantial resources on monitoring client behaviour and may thereby be driven to incremental innovations. When a completely new product or new service is developed, this is a structural innovation. Structural innovation will not take place in an organisation with the Chameleon business model. Where it does occur, the business model transforms into the Innovator. The Innovator network no longer evolves step-by-step. Usually such examples involve spin-out management, as the nature of governance of the Chameleon organisation does not match the governance of that innovation.

Business Models: It's still about Money, for the Moment

In a conversation with Ronald Kasteel, chairman of the Board of Ordina, a Dutch system integrator, we discussed the business model concept at a deeper level and explored the meaning of the types of model in his daily practice. In his view, nothing fundamental will change. No matter how inspirational the words from the language of the 'emotion-economy', the underlying motivation remains money making. This means that traditional business principles still apply. Customers and suppliers will continue to build and maintain relations on the basis of mutual interest. These relations do change and mature. They revolve increasingly around trust, adding value to the business processes of the client, and cooperative relations with the client become solidified. Customer-supplier relations therefore are confronted with fundamentally different expectations.

In the IT service sector companies increasingly actively try to meet the demands of clients through the offering of customisation. Kasteel asserts that aspiring multiple values is self-evident. In his organisation values other than just making money play important roles. Being able to use a client as a reference, having a sense of pride concerning the employees, network relations and enthusiasm among employees are examples. Some of these values belong both in the realm of reciprocal values, and in the realm of human resources. Ordina, according to Kasteel, is a 'real Chameleon organisation'. Aside from the delivery of IT capacity (Ordina's original core business), the company increasingly engages in the provision of integrated solutions for customers. Customer requirements drive the business at all times, along with healthy principles of business economics, such as a strive for profits.

Kasteel is resolute concerning the other two ideal types of business models. Most companies will reason from the perspective of the Chameleon business model. Activities may be developed that match the Innovator or the Foyer, but these are ultimately focused on the strengthening of the Chameleon. The involvement of Ordina with Parents Online, a community where young parents share ideas and thoughts about parenthood and children, is a good example. This virtual community closely resembles the Foyer model. For Ordina this was an experiment, designed to generate innovative applications that might be of relevance for the organisation and for their customers. This means that the virtual community is more a 'vehicle' for the achievement of innovation rather than a fundamentally new business model.

Currently no 'drivers' can be predicted that might topple his vision on business models. A change in mindset about customer relations is within reach. Cooperation with customers and the sharing of knowledge with them is of growing importance. There is already intensive knowledge sharing in some larger Dutch companies, supported by the implementation of IT. Knowledge sharing with competitors, on the other hand, is not evident. Knowledge is of vital importance for competitive advantage.

Kasteel does not believe that companies will 'dedicate' themselves to Foyer-like business models on a large scale. Elements from the emotion-economy, however, will increasingly be influential in bricks and mortar business models, oriented towards straight 'money-making'. He also expects that, in the future, all models will diverge towards a 'richer' Chameleon model; a business model in which the strategy of money making is supported by virtual communities in the form of Foyer and knowledge sharing networks that realise innovation.

(Innovator)

DYNAMICS OF THE INNOVATOR

The Innovator is a business model which is always a temporary configuration of parties. A potential movement towards other business models (such as the Foyer or Chameleon) is inherent.

INNOVATOR–CHAMELEON

Chapter 5 explained that in the Innovator model the commercial exploitation of an innovation is often delegated or sold to organisations that have opted for a traditional business model or for the Chameleon business model. In the latter case, new products or services will be offered to the customers on the basis of personalisation. The Innovator then disbands, or occupies itself with new innovations. Innovating organisations may naturally decide to exploit the innovation themselves, as BIBIT does in the text below, but in that case the core business model will change. The emphasis in the choice of supporting IT-applications will shift from communication, learning and knowledge sharing, to process control and integration of information to support the new strategy, governance and processes. An Innovator network that follows this path then moves in the direction of the Chameleon model.

Life Cycle of the Innovator Organisation

In a conversation with Joost Schuijff, founder and CEO of BIBIT, we focused on the Innovator business model. BIBIT was founded in 1997 by Joost Schuijff and two co-founders. The company's primary activity is the facilitation of financial transactions of customers for companies, such as webshops. It handles the processing and completion of transactions with more than 75 different methods of payment.

BIBIT started as an Innovator. The founder had completed assignments in the field of IT for various Dutch banks for years, as an independent consultant. This meant that he possessed not only knowledge of methods of payments and IT-systems of banks, but he also had access to a network in the financial world. The idea of facilitating Internet payments represented a time specialist service in the financial market. In those days, the financing of Internet start-ups or related companies by venture capitalists was no problem.

Trust remains an essential aspect in the BIBIT network. Outsourcing an important part of the customer process (payment) to a third party, puts the customer in a vulnerable position. When the organisation has proved itself trustworthy and established a loyal client base, trust becomes part of the entry barrier for competitors in the market. Relations are transformed into partnerships.

Joost Schuijff considers a business model as the way an organisation makes money. In the case of BIBIT, the innovative way in which money is made forms the basis of the company. One of the founders dreams is to be able to offer a scalable solution for accepting payments, that can be automated. The scalability of the solution and the repeat nature of the transactions will lead to a low cost-price. Future business models, according to Joost Schuijff, will be dominated by process improvements and cost optimisation. The phase in the economy we currently find ourselves in and the enhanced potential of new technology encourage ever more scalable activities. The cost of extra transactions, from a certain point on, becomes practically zero.

In the beginning the founder was so close to the 'business' that he himself was often at the forefront of new developments, new products, new services or new markets. As the company grew, he had increasingly less time for these activities. There are now several so-called active 'business developers' in the BIBIT organisation, who play a leading part in product development and innovation.

'As a small innovative company grows, the need for fixed procedures and methods grows with it', says Joost Schuijff. This does not benefit its creative capacity. However, there is no other option. With expansion comes the necessity for a more robust organisational form. A management team was appointed to lead the company, consisting of employees who were hired to guide the company during its period of rapid growth. It could be that the appointment of a management team is a signal for the transformation of the Innovator towards a different business model, such as the Chameleon. The organisation of BIBIT indeed exhibits nowadays most of the characteristics of a Chameleon model.

According to Joost Schuijff, the Innovator is never blessed with long life. Innovation can only thrive in small organisations, with few layers of managements. An Innovator draws certain kinds of people, where the emphasis lies in communication and individual responsibility; in an environment where inspired leadership, rather than management, is required. If an innovation becomes a success in the market, the organisation will naturally move towards a Chameleon model, or even become a traditional organisation. In such a case, structural innovation is rarely possibly anymore. Incremental innovation, on the other hand, may still take place. A small core group of the original Innovator network may continue independently in order to realise new innovations. Thus, it seems that there is an innovation cycle repeatedly ending with the successful launch of the innovative product or service.

INNOVATOR–FOYER

The Innovator makes use of all kinds of virtual communities, from communities of practice to communities of interest. An important development in this context towards the Foyer business model is the emergence of user communities that begin to innovate without the actual involvement of the original producer organisations (Von Hippel 2000).

The infusion of new information technologies in customer-firm interactions has redefined the roles customers can play in value creation and product innovation. Several companies (e.g. Microsoft, Hewlett-Packard, Procter & Gamble, Volvo, Samsung and Peugeot) have established online or virtual product communities, virtual product prototyping and testing centres, and other virtual product forums to facilitate rich interactions between customers and firms as well as among customers themselves, and to involve customers in varied value creation activities ranging from the design and development of new products to product testing and customer support.

Sony recently set up a website to support gamers interested in exploring and developing new types of games that could be played on the Sony Playstation. It quickly attracted 10,000 participants, a number that vastly exceeds the number of in-house and contract developers creating games for the Playstation. It is possible that, taken individually, in-house developers are technically more skilled than most user-developers. But the user-developer community mobilised by Sony has a huge diversity of interests and skills. Sony's vice president of third-party R&D, Phil Harrison, thinks that some of them will come up with 'some radically new forms of creativity that will break the conventions that are holding back the business today.'

(Von Hippel 2000)

DYNAMICS OF THE FOYER

In the Foyer business model there is also a natural movement in the direction of the two other models.

FOYER–CHAMELEON

The transition from the Foyer to the Chameleon model may take place if one or more participants decide to offer products or services themselves. These often involve products or services that appear to do well with the participants in the Foyer. In this state of transition, one often finds a combination of both Foyer and Chameleon and the exploitation of the opportunities of both business models, depending on the goals that are set. In practice this will not occur very often, since participants engage in the community with a different intention and a different mentality.

As Ronald Kasteel points out, in most cases we will see a reverse trend, with organisations moving from the Chameleon business model, to join one or more Foyer communities. After all, customers' interests, such as access to and reliability of the information, can easily be traced and promoted through the Foyer. The offer of products, customised to individual customer demands, can then be marketed through the Chameleon business model.

FOYER–INNOVATOR

The Foyer model clearly emphasises information exchange, knowledge sharing and co-operation. Many activities are primarily focused on the intensification of relations and the strengthening of the community, but participants in a Foyer

Business Models and Three Worlds

Rik Maes is Professor of Information and Communication management, Business Studies Department, at the Faculty of Economic Sciences and Business Studies at the Universiteit van Amsterdam. In our conversation with him we asked for his opinion on business models and about perspectives for the future (from an academic point of view).

He distinguishes two dimensions of the business model concept. Firstly, a business model is a combination of what used to be called 'strategy' and of the way the company is designed. The second dimension concerns the new ways to deal with the 'new economy', which are dependent on IT and knowledge on the one hand and emotional values on the other hand.

Maes suggests that business models might best be examined by assuming three worlds: the physical world (the world of the tangibles, money and products, the doing), the informational world (the world of information and knowledge, the thinking and knowing), and the emotional world (the world of experience, the feeling and wanting).

All these three worlds should be addressed in the business model that is selected by an organisation. For example, take the business model of the Dutch newspaper 'De Telegraaf'. This ought to emphasise heavily the emotional world, since the choice of the readers of this paper is driven by certain emotions. However, the managers of this paper talk about their business model in terms of the physical world (the product paper, money and shareholders) and the informational world (digital papers, exclusives and so on.). Consequently the emotional aspect is ignored, while it ought to be very important and because of this, important opportunities are missed.

A business model that revolves only around the physical and the informational world is not a business model, but an automaton, according to Rik Maes.

For instance, he asserts that the design principle of knowledge management, which is paramount to the Innovator model, will not be established as long as we consider it from the informational stance as purely a cognitive matter. After all, knowledge management has a lot to do with emotional and cultural issues such as sharing and interacting. And yet this is hardly ever reflected in the concepts. The same goes for customer relationship management, which is an important IT-application in the Chameleon model. Companies invest millions in CRM, having closed the offices located close to their customers. But if you only focus on knowledge management, CRM and so on, as isolated activities, then your efforts will amount to nothing. The same is true of the digital economy. It has recently become clear that it holds no connections with the physical world, and it is therefore no surprise that a crisis occurred.

The three types of business models in this book each emphasise one of the three worlds. The Chameleon revolves mostly around the physical world, the Innovator around the informational/knowledge world, and the Foyer around the emotional world. It is therefore not very surprising that the real money is made primarily by the Chameleon. But where previously Chameleons with an aspiration for expansion tended to move towards innovations (thus towards the Innovator), you can now see primarily a shift towards the Foyer. Clear changes can be identified in that area. As for the future, Maes suspects that the three types of business model will converge to a middle ground. This is because, separately, none of the three business models sufficiently acknowledges all three worlds. Perhaps then a circle, on which the three types of business model and their mixed forms move, would be a better illustration of reality than the triangle with its sharp edges.

often also create a context from which innovative activities may emerge. When the focus on innovations starts to dominate, a transition may begin towards the Innovator business model. Incidentally, this need not imply that the entire Foyer network will follow this transition. It may be that only the part of the network that occupies itself emphatically with innovation will shift towards the Innovator model.

In this dynamic development, those who choose the Innovator business model will need to ensure that the values of the Foyer are not lost. This can be achieved for instance by placing the innovational activities in a so-called 'value network' (Tapscott 1998). Value is generated in such a network (of which competitors, costumers, suppliers and other stakeholders are part) by means of a continuously changing open structure. It is a model that stimulates flexibility, innovation, entrepreneurship and pro-active abilities. In Toronto, the Virtual Corporation makes available a network and other services, in order to allow independent advisors and software developers to engage in projects as partners.

A Foyer that focuses (in part) on innovational activities will probably never fully transform into the Innovator business model. It is far more likely that a business model emerges that is a combination of both types. This business model will continue to use the relations that were established in the Foyer. This is indeed necessary, since new information flows will originate between the Innovator network, their customers and the relationships between them, that in turn will be the sources of new ideas, new product concepts and so on.

A VISION OF THE FUTURE

In this last section we wish to reflect on the interviews and provide our vision on the future. To this end we pose two questions:

Is a combination of business models possible?

The answer to this question is twofold: from a business perspective the answer tends to be negative, but for a specific organisation the answer can be more positive.

We believe that for every business, a strategic choice for *one* of the three business model types should be made. Combinations where two or more business models are of equal significance may cause serious problems in the business. Governance, the (control of the) processes and the function of the accompanying IT differ for each model to such an extent that it may be simply unfeasible to maintain more than one business model within a single business. The complexity of the whole becomes too great to be managed. On the other hand, once an organisation has chosen a dominant business model, a number of aspects within it may be adopted that are characteristic of the other two. An example is found in the interview with Kasteel, in which he points to the involvement of Ordina with the community Parents Online (a Dutch website where parents discuss the challenges they face while raising their children).

A specific organisation on the other hand may indeed opt for more than one business model. The reason for this is that organisations are often active in multiple 'businesses', which require different business models for the organisation to be effective. These are often organised along business unit lines. From the perspective of the organisation this has substantial implications for management. In the interviews we discussed combinations of business models both from the academic point of view and from a practical business point of view. It became clear that it is very important to realise that a combination of business models will make new demands on management. A focal point of this book is that the governance of each of the three types differs fundamentally. This does not imply that a combination is impossible, but it does mean that organisations should be aware of the consequences of various governance forms in the same organisation (or network).

Organisations will need to take explicit action to balance the various approaches to governance, which come with the various business models. This should be paramount when selecting a business model. It is for this reason that we explicitly state: *In the future, the principle task of management will be the management of the interfaces between the internal organisation, the innovating network and the communities in which the organisation exists.*

The second question is:

What does the future hold?

At the moment, organisations make money with the Chameleon model. The interviews with Kasteel and Schuijff confirm this notion, although the anticipation of and reaction to developments such as virtual communities, on the one hand, and the necessity of creating space for innovations, on the other hand, are also evident.

In our vision, the image sketched out by Maes is indicative for the future. The three worlds will be distinguishable in every business, but we believe that the emphasis will shift from the physical to the worlds of the ideas and the emotions. The growing importance of knowledge and innovation and the enormous speed and intensity with which communities evolve, driven by a sincere desire for involvement, are reason enough to suspect that the other two 'points' of the triangle will grow in relevance. Although only time will tell whether or not these models will overtake the Chameleon model in importance, there are now plenty of signs to predict a gain in territory for these two business models.

One thing is certain. When choosing a business model, you must consider the direction you wish or need to take in order to maximise the (tangible or intangible) returns of the activities you want to engage in. The typology presented in this book, with its underlying considerations, may be a helpful guide.

We have not attempted to present a fully elaborated typology, which managers could apply directly to the implementation of one or more types. The purpose of the typology we have described is to encourage reflection about the future and about the consequences of choosing a particular business model. The value of the typology lies in the fact that organisations can find clues for the kind of transformation they are seeking. The description of these types of business model may serve to prompt a dialogue, if for instance one decides to move more towards innovation and/or authenticity and/or customisation.

The question of where all this leads is still very much open ended. The book therefore closes with the same question we asked in the first chapter:

What will your new business model be?

Bibliography

Abraham, J. L. and Knight, D. J. (2001), Strategic innovation, leveraging creative action for more profitable growth, *Strategy and Leadership*, vol. 29, no. 1, pp. 21–27.

Amidon, D. M. (1997), *Innovation Strategy for the Knowledge Economy: The Ken Awakening*, UK: Butterworth-Heinemann, subsidiary of Reed Elsevier.

Amit, R. and Schoemaker, P. (1993), Strategic assets and organizational rent, *Strategic Management Journal*, vol. 14.

Amit, R. and Zott, C. (2000), Value drivers of e-commerce business models, *Knowledge @ Wharton*, 30 July.

Applegate, L. M. (2001), E-business Models: Making Sense of the Internet Business Landscape, in *Information Technology and the Future Enterprise: New Models for Managers*. G. DeSanctis. Upper Saddle River, NJ: Prentice Hall.

Arthur, W. B. (2002), Is the information revolution dead? *Business 2.0*, www.business2.com/May

Bambury, P. (2001), *A Taxonomy of Internet Commerce*, www.firstmonday.dk/issues/issue3_10/bambury/

Barney, J. B. (1991), Firm resources and sustained competitive advantage, *Journal of Management*, vol. 17.

Brandenburger, A. M. and Nalebuff, B. J. (1997), The added-value theory of business. *Strategy & Business*, fourth quarter, www.strategy-business.com/briefs/97412/index.html

Canter, L. A. and Siegel, M. S. (1995), *How to Make a Fortune on the Information Superhighway: Everyone's Guerilla Guide to Marketing on the Internet and Other On line E-services*, New York: HarperCollins Publishers.

Castells, M. (1998), *The Information Age, Economy, Society and Culture, Volume 1: The Rise of the Network Society*. Massachusetts, USA and Oxford, UK: Blackwell Publishers Inc.

Castells, M. (1998), *The Information Age, Economy, Society and culture, volume III: The end of Millennium*, Massachesetts, USA and Oxford, UK: Blackwell Publishers Inc.

Centers for IBM e-business Innovation (2000), *Models Made E: What Business are You in?*, New York: IBM, Somers.

Chesbrough, H. and Rosenbloom, R. S. (2002), The role of the business model in capturing value from innovation: Evidence from Xerox Corporation's technology spin-off companies, *Industrial and Corporate Change*, vol. 11, no 3, pp. 529–556.

Christensen, C. (1997), *The Innovator's Dilemma: When New Technologies Cause Great Firms to Fail*, Boston: Harvard Business School Press.

Clark, P. and Staunton, N. (1989), *Innovation in Technology and Organization*, London-New York: Routledge.

Dörflinger, M. and Marxt, C. (2001), Mass customization – neue potenziale durch kundenindividuelle massenproduktion, *ioManagement*, no. 3, pp. 86–93.

Drucker, P. (2001), *The Essential Drucker*, Oxford, UK: Butterworth-Heinemann.

Dubosson-Torbay, M., Osterwalder, A. and Pigeneur, Y. (2002), E-business model design, classification, and measurements, *Thunderbird International Business Review*, vol. 44, no. 1, pp. 5–23.

Dutta, S. and Segev, A. (1999), *Business Transformation on the Internet*. Working Paper 98-WP-1035, Jan, http://haas.berkeley.edu/citm/wp-1035.pdf

Dyer, J. H. and Singh, H. (1998), The relational view: cooperative strategy and sources of interorganizational competitive advantage, *Academy of Management Review*, vol. 23, no. 4.

Ethiraj, S., Guler, I. and Singh, H. (2000), The impact of Internet and electronic technologies on firms and its implications for competitive advantage, *Knowledge @ Wharton*, http://johnmolson.concordia.ca/gkersten/ec_papers/models/00Ethiraj_models.pdf

Fernback, J. and Thompson, B. (2000), *Virtual Communities: Abort, Retry, Failure?* March, www.well.com/user/hlr/texts/Vccivil.html. A version of this paper, entitled 'Computer-Mediated Communication and the American Collectivity:

The Dimensions of Community Within Cyberspace,' was presented at the annual convention of the International Communication Association, Albuquerque, New Mexico, May 1995.

Frohman, A. L. (1998), Building a culture for innovation, *Research Technology Magazine*, Mar–Apr, vol. 41, no. 2.

Galbreath, J. (1999), Customer relationship leadership: a leadership and motivation model for the twenty-first century business, *TQM Magazine*, vol. 11, no. 3, pp. 161–171.

Gardner & Associates Consulting (2000), *Mass Customization: ERP Implementation Challenges and What to Do About it*, www.dealconsulting.com/operations/mc.html

Gordijn J., Osterwalder, A. and Pigneur, Y. (2005), *Comparing two business model ontologies for designing e-business models and value constellations*. Proceedings of the 18e Bled eConference, Bled, Slovenia, 6–8 June. www.hec.unil.ch/yp/Pub/05-Bled.pdf

Green, H. (1999), Throw out your old business model: online business are whole different animals. It pays to be adaptable. *Businessweek Online*, 22 March. www.businessweek.com/1999/99_12/b3621006.htm

Gulati, R. and Garino, J. (2000), Get the right mix of bricks and clicks, *Harvard Business Review*, May–June.

Hagel, H. and Armstrong, A. G. (1997), *Net Gain: Expanding Markets Through Virtual Communities*, Boston: Harvard Business School Press.

Hauschildt, J. (1997), *Innovations Management*, München: Verlag Vahlen.

Hedman, J. and Kalling, T. (2003), The business model concept: theoretical underpinnings and empirical illustrations, *European Journal of Information Systems, Journal of the Operational Research Society*, vol. 12, no 1, pp. 49–59.

Hippel, E. von, Thomke, S. and Sonnack, M. (1999) *Creating Breakthrough Innovations at 3M*, http://www.leaduser.com/documents/3M_Breakthrough_Article.html

Hippel, E. von (2000), *Creating Market-connected Innovations*, June, www.smeal.psu.edu/lsbm/publications/nuggets/membersJune2000/hippel.pdf

Hippel, E. von (2001), *Interview*, www.cio.com/archive/101500/something_content.html

Jagersma, P., Pijl, P. v.d. and Raaijmakers, M. (2001), On the way towards a new business model (in Dutch: Op weg naar een nieuw businessmodel), *Holland/Belgium Management Review*, Mar–Apr.

Jansen, R. M. (2002), *E-formulas, Strategy Design Success*, Veenendaal: Universal Press.

Jansen, W., Steenbakkers, G. C. A. and Jägers, H. P. M. (1999), Knowledge management and organization design, pp. 181–195, in Malhotra, Y. (ed.), *Knowledge Management and Virtual Organizations*, Hershey: Idea Group Publishing.

Jansen, W., Steenbakkers, G. C. A. and Jägers, H. P. M. (2002), The virtual corporation, balancing between identity and innovation, pp. 43–60, in Franke, U. (ed.), *Managing the Virtual Web Organization in the 21st Century: Issues and Challenges*, Hershey: Idea Group Publishing.

Jarvenpaa, S. L. and Shaw, T. R. (1998), *Global virtual teams: integrating models of trust*, Proceedings of the VONET Workshop, Bern, 27–28 April.

Jarvenpaa, S. L. and Leidner, D. E. (1998), Communication and Trust in Global Virtual Teams, *JCMC* vol. 3, no. 4, www.ascusc.org/jcmc/vol3/issue4/jarvenpaa.html

Kalthoff, O., Nonaka, I. and Nueno, P. (1997), *The Light and the Shadow, How Breakthrough Innovation is Shaping European Business*, Oxford: Capstone Publishing Limited.

Kaplan, S. and Sawhney, M. (2000), *B2B e-commerce hubs: towards a taxonomy of business models*, www.mohansawhney.com/articles/linked/B2B.pdf

Kogut, B. and Zander, U. (1996), What firms do? Coordination, identity and learning, *Organization Science*, vol. 7, no. 5, pp. 502–518.

Kollock, P. (1999), The economies of online cooperation: Gifts and public goods in cyberspace, pp. 220–239, in Smith, M. A. and Kollock, P., *Communities in Cyberspace*, London: Routledge.

Laat, P. de (2000), Technological Innovation, *Operations Research/Management Science*, vol. 40, no. 1.

Lagace, M. (2000), What is an internet business model, ask a health care professional, *Harvard Business School Working Knowledge for Business Leader*, 26 June, http://hbswk.hbs.edu/pubitem.jhtml?id=1577&sid=-1&t=special_reports

Leifer, R., McDermott, C. M., Colarelli O'Connor, G., Peters, L. S., Rice, M. P. and Veryzer, R. W. (2002), *Radical Innovation: How Mature Companies Can Outsmart Upstarts*, Boston: Havard Business School Press.

Levy, M. (2001), *E-volve-or-Die.com*, Indiana: New Riders Publishing.

Lipnack, J. and Stamps, J. (2000), *Virtual Teams*, www.managementroundtable. com/PDBPR/lipnack_stamp.html

Magretta, J. (1998), The power of virtual integration: An interview with Dell Computer's Michael Dell, *Harvard Business Review*, vol. 76, no. 2, pp. 72–85.

Magretta, J. (2002), Why business models matter, *Harvard Business Review*, May, pp. 86–92.

Malhotra, Y. (2000), Knowledge management for e-business performance: advancing information strategy to 'Internet Time', *Information Strategy*, vol. 16, no. 4, pp. 5–16.

McKnight, D. H., Cummings, L. L. and Chervany, N. L. (1998), Initial trust formation in new organizational relationships, *Academy of Management Review*, vol. 23, no. 3, pp. 473–490.

McMaster, M. D. (1998), *Organising for Innovation, Technology and Intelligent Capacity*, WWW Virtual Library on KM (Knowledge Management), www. brint.com/km/mcmaster/confer.htm

Melger, H. B. (2001), *Virtual Communities, An Exploration for Clarification*, University of Amsterdam: Final Thesis: Business Information Systems.

Miles, R. E., Snow, C. C. and Miles, G. (2000), The future organization. *Long Range Planning*, vol. 33, no. 3, pp. 300–321.

Nonaka, I. and Takeuchi, H. (1995), *The Knowledge Creating Company*, New York: Oxford University Press.

Peppers, D. Rogers, M. and Dorf, B. (1999), Is your company ready for one-to-one marketing?, *Harvard Business Review*, Jan–Feb, pp. 151–160.

Peteraf, M. A. (1993), The cornerstones of competitive advantage: A resource based view, *Strategic Management Journal*, vol. 14.

Picard, R. G. (2000), Changing Business Models for Online Content Services. Their Implications for Multimedia and Other Content Producers, Turku School of Economics and Business Administration, Finland, 2000, *JMM*, vol. 2, no. 2.

Pine, B. J. and Gilmore, J. H. (1999), *The Experience Economy: Work Is Theater and Every Business a Stage*, Boston: Harvard Business School Press.

Porter, M. E. (1985), *Competitive Advantage*, New York: Free Press.

Porter, M. E. (2001), Strategy and the internet, *Harvard Business Review*, vol. 3, no. 1.

Prahalad, C. K. and Ramaswany, V. (2000), Co-opting customer competence, *Harvard Business Review*, vol. 78, no. 1, pp. 79–87.

Preece, J. (2000), *Online Communities: Designing Usability and Supporting Sociability*, Hoboken, New Jersey: John Wiley & Sons Inc.

Quinn, J. B., Baruch, J. J. and Zien, K. A. (1996), Software-based innovation, *Sloan Management Review*, vol. 37, no. 4.

Rappa, M. (2000), *Business Models on the Web*, NC State University.

Rappa, M. (2003), *Managing the Digital Enterprise: Business Models on the Web*, http://digitalenterprise.org/models/models.html (retrieved 5 April 2003).

Rheingold, H. (1993), *Virtual Community: Homesteading on the Virtual Frontier*. Reading: Addison Wesley, www.rheingold.com/vc/book.

Ryan, J. and Whiteman, N. (2000), *Community Building: Good or Bad for Ad Revenues?*, ClickZ Network, 28 August, http://clickz.com/cgi-bin/gt/article.html?article=2305

Sawhney, M. and Kaplan, S. (1999), *B2B E-commerce Hubs: Towards a Taxonomy of Business Models*, Northwestern University, www.eyefortransport.com/archive/kaplan22.pdf

Scharmer, C. O. (2000), *Self Transcending Knowledge*. www.ottoscharmer.com/STK.pdf

Shapiro, C. and Varian, H. R. (1999), *Information Rules: A Strategic Guide to the Network Economy*, Boston: Harvard Business School Press.

Shubar A. and Lechner, U. (2004), *The public WLAN market and its business models*. In J. Gricar (ed), eGlobal, 17th Bled ECommerce Conference 2004.

Taylor, T. (1992), *The Ethics of Authenticity*, Boston: Harvard University Press.

Tapscott, D. (1998), *Blueprint to the Digital Economy*, New York: McGraw-Hill.

Telematica Instituut (1999), *The Merits Approach*, https://doc.telin.nl/dscgi/ds.py/Get/File-49/D111.pdf

Timmers, P. (1998), Business models for electronic markets, *International Journal of Electronic Markets*, vol. 98, no. 2, pp. 3–8.

Tovstiga, G. and Fantner, E. J. (2000), Implications of the dynamics of the new networked economy for e-business start-ups: the case of Philips' Access Point, *Internet Research*, vol. 10, no. 5, pp. 459–470.

Treacy, M. and Wiersema, F. (1995), *The Discipline of Market Leaders*, New York: HarperCollins Publishers.

Tucker, R. B. (2001), Innovation, the new core competency, *Strategy and Leadership*, vol. 29, no. 1, pp. 11–14.

Ulwick, T. and Eisenhauer, J. A. (2000), *I Managing Innovation with a Customer's Perception of Value*, www.strategyn.com/whitePapers

Ulwick, T. and Eisenhauer, J. A. (2000), *II Customers do not Know What They Want. Or do They?*, www.strategyn.com/whitePapers

Volberda, H. W. (1998), *Continuous strategic innovation: competitive advantage in the 21st century* (in Dutch: Blijvend strategisch vernieuwen; concurreren in de 21e eeuw), Inaugural Lecture, Kluwer, Deventer.

De Vries, E. J. (2003), *ICT Enabled Distribution of Services: Service Positioning Strategy, Front Office Information and Multi-channeling*, dissertation, University of Amsterdam.

Weill, P. and Vitale, M. R. (2001), *Place to Space. Migrating to E-business Models*, Boston: Harvard Business School Press.

Weill, P., Malone, T. W., D'Urso, V. T., Herman, G. and Woerner, S. (2005), *Do Some Business Models Perform Better than Others?*, A Study of the 1000 Largest US Firms, MIT Center for Coordination Science Working Paper No. 226 http://ccs.mit.edu/papers/pdf/wp226.pdf

Wernerfelt, B. (1984), A resource-based view of the firm, *Strategic Management Journal*, vol. 5.

Wilde, E. de and Brenk, M. van (2002), *Down to Earth. E-commerce strategies after the hype* (in Dutch: E-commercestrategieën na de hype), Amsterdam: Prentice Hall.

Williamson, O. E. (1975), *Markets and Hierarchies, Analysis and Antitrust Implications*, New York: Macmillan.

Index

About the Authors

Wendy Jansen is research fellow at the Economic Faculty of the Universiteit van Amsterdam and management consultant at Trias. She is the author of over 100 books and articles on the design of organisations, networks and business models. Currently she is studying the design of organisations which are implementing process management and the images which are underlying this implementation. She may be contacted at wendyjansen@trias.nl.

Wilchard Steenbakkers is Principle Consultant at Ordina. He has many years of experience in consulting on organisational and informational issues in profit and not for profit organisations. He has published books and articles on knowledge management, organisational change, organisational networks and business models. Currently, he has been involved in projects concerning IT Governance and Application Portfolio Management. He may be contacted at wilchard.steenbakkers@ordina.nl.

Hans Jägers taught for many years as a Professor of the Faculty of Economic Sciences and Business Studies of the Universiteit van Amsterdam (The Netherlands). Also, he has been the dean of the academic faculty of the Netherlands Royal Military Academy. His many areas of published research include organisational design, knowledge management, information management, networks and business models. Currently he is CEO of Aeqos Consulting. He may be contacted at h.jagers@parelnet.nl.